CAMBRIDGE LIBRARY COLLECTION

Books of enduring scholarly value

History

The books reissued in this series include accounts of historical events and movements by eye-witnesses and contemporaries, as well as landmark studies that assembled significant source materials or developed new historiographical methods. The series includes work in social, political and military history on a wide range of periods and regions, giving modern scholars ready access to influential publications of the past.

Rights of Man. Part the Second. Combining Principle and Practice

A major actor in the American Revolution, English intellectual Thomas Paine (1737–1809) is remembered especially for his pamphlet *Common Sense* (1776; also reissued in this series), which advocates America's independence from Great Britain. A dedicated radical, Paine went on to lend his support to the French Revolution. In 1791, he published *Rights of Man* in response to Burke's *Reflections on the Revolution in France* (1790), a condemnation of the events in France. First published in 1792, this book is a continuation of *Rights of Man*. While the first volume was a passionate rebuttal of Burke's argument, this book – reissued here in its second edition – develops concrete measures for political reform, proposing novel concepts such as political representation and tax reform to benefit the poor. Widely circulated because of its low price, the book proved immensely influential, and resulted in indictments for seditious libel for Paine and his editor.

T0351966

Cambridge University Press has long been a pioneer in the reissuing of out-of-print titles from its own backlist, producing digital reprints of books that are still sought after by scholars and students but could not be reprinted economically using traditional technology. The Cambridge Library Collection extends this activity to a wider range of books which are still of importance to researchers and professionals, either for the source material they contain, or as landmarks in the history of their academic discipline.

Drawing from the world-renowned collections in the Cambridge University Library and other partner libraries, and guided by the advice of experts in each subject area, Cambridge University Press is using state-of-the-art scanning machines in its own Printing House to capture the content of each book selected for inclusion. The files are processed to give a consistently clear, crisp image, and the books finished to the high quality standard for which the Press is recognised around the world. The latest print-on-demand technology ensures that the books will remain available indefinitely, and that orders for single or multiple copies can quickly be supplied.

The Cambridge Library Collection brings back to life books of enduring scholarly value (including out-of-copyright works originally issued by other publishers) across a wide range of disciplines in the humanities and social sciences and in science and technology.

Rights of Man.
Part the Second.
Combining Principle
and Practice

THOMAS PAINE

CAMBRIDGE
UNIVERSITY PRESS

CAMBRIDGE UNIVERSITY PRESS

Cambridge, New York, Melbourne, Madrid, Cape Town,
Singapore, São Paolo, Delhi, Mexico City

Published in the United States of America by Cambridge University Press, New York

www.cambridge.org
Information on this title: www.cambridge.org/9781108045469

© in this compilation Cambridge University Press 2012

This edition first published 1792
This digitally printed version 2012

ISBN 978-1-108-04546-9 Paperback

This book reproduces the text of the original edition. The content and language reflect
the beliefs, practices and terminology of their time, and have not been updated.

Cambridge University Press wishes to make clear that the book, unless originally published
by Cambridge, is not being republished by, in association or collaboration with, or
with the endorsement or approval of, the original publisher or its successors in title.

RIGHTS OF MAN.

PART

THE SECOND.

COMBINING

PRINCIPLE AND PRACTICE.

BY

THOMAS PAINE,

SECRETARY FOR FOREIGN AFFAIRS TO CONGRESS IN THE
AMERICAN WAR, AND AUTHOR OF THE WORK ENTITLED
COMMON SENSE; AND THE FIRST PART OF THE RIGHTS
OF MAN.

THE SECOND EDITION.

LONDON:

PRINTED FOR J. S. JORDAN, NO. 166, FLEET-STREET.

1792.

TO

M. DE LA FAYETTE.

AFTER an acquaintance of nearly fifteen years, in difficult situations in America, and various consultations in Europe, I feel a pleasure in presenting to you this small treatise, in gratitude for your services to my beloved America, and as a testimony of my esteem for the virtues, public and private, which I know you to possess.

The only point upon which I could ever discover that we differed, was not as to principles of government, but as to time. For my own part, I think it equally as injurious to good principles to permit them to linger, as to push them on too fast. That which you suppose accomplishable in fourteen or fifteen years, I may believe practicable in a much shorter period. Mankind, as it appears to me, are always ripe enough to understand their true interest, provided it be presented clearly to their understanding, and that in a manner not to create suspicion by any thing like self-design, nor offend by assuming too much. Where we would wish to reform we must not reproach.

When the American revolution was established, I felt a disposition to sit serenely down and enjoy

the

the calm. It did not appear to me that any ob_ject could afterwards arife great enough to make me quit tranquillity, and feel as I had felt before. But when principle, and not place, is the energetic caufe of action, a man, I find, is every where the fame.

I am now once more in the public world; and as I have not a right to contemplate on fo many years of remaining life as you have, I am re-folved to labour as faft as I can; and as I am anxious for your aid and your company, I wifh you to haften your principles, and overtake me.

If you make a campaign the enfuing fpring, which it is moft probable there will be no occafion for, I will come and join you. Should the campaign commence, I hope it will terminate in the extinction of German defpotifm, and in eftablifh-ing the freedom of all Germany. When France fhall be furrounded with revolutions, fhe will be in peace and fafety, and her taxes, as well as thofe of Germany, will confequently become lefs.

Your fincere,

Affectionate Friend,

THOMAS PAINE.

London, Feb. 9, 1792.

PREFACE.

WHEN I began the chapter entitled the *"Conclusion"* in the former part of the RIGHTS OF MAN, publifhed laft year, it was my intention to have extended it to a greater length; but in cafting the whole matter in my mind which I wifhed to add, I found that I muft either make the work too bulky, or contract my plan too much. I therefore brought it to a clofe as foon as the fubject would admit, and referved what I had further to fay to another opportunity.

Several other reafons contributed to produce this determination. I wifhed to know the manner in which a work, written in a ftyle of thinking and expreffion different to what had been cuftomary in England, would be received before I proceeded farther. A great field was opening to the view of mankind by means of the French Revolution. Mr. Burke's outrageous oppofition thereto brought the controverfy into England. He attacked principles which he knew (from information) I would conteft with him, becaufe they are principles I believe to be good, and which I have contributed to eftablifh, and conceive myfelf bound to defend. Had he not urged the controverfy, I had moft probably been a filent man.

Anothe

Another reason for deferring the remainder of the work was, that Mr. Burke promised in his first publication to renew the subject at another opportunity, and to make a comparison of what he called the English and French Constitutions. I therefore held myself in reserve for him. He has published two works since, without doing this; which he certainly would not have omitted, had the comparison been in his favour.

In his last work, " *His appeal from the new to* " *the old Whigs*," he has quoted about ten pages from the *Rights of Man*, and having given himself the trouble of doing this, says, " he shall not at-" tempt in the smallest degree to refute them," meaning the principles therein contained. I am enough acquainted with Mr. Burke to know, that he would if he could. But instead of contesting them, he immediately after consoles himself with saying, that " he has done his part."—He has not done his part. He has not performed his promise of a comparison of constitutions. He started the controversy, he gave the challenge, and has fled from it; and he is now a *case in point* with his own opinion, that, " *the age of chivalry is gone!*"

The title, as well as the substance of his last work, his " *Appeal*," is his condemnation. Principles must stand on their own merits, and if they are good they certainly will. To put them under the shelter of other men's authority, as Mr. Burke has done, serves to bring them into suspicion. Mr. Burke is not very fond of dividing his honours, but in this case he is artfully dividing the disgrace.

But

But who are thofe to whom Mr. Burke has made his appeal? A fet of childifh thinkers and half-way politicians born in the laft century; men who went no farther with any principle than as it fuited their purpofe as a party; the nation was always left out of the queftion; and this has been the character of every party from that day to this. The nation fees nothing in fuch works, or fuch politics worthy its attention. A little matter will move a party, but it muft be fomething great that moves a nation.

Though I fee nothing in Mr. Burke's Appeal worth taking much notice of, there is, however, one expreffion upon which I fhall offer a few remarks.—After quoting largely from the *Rights of Man*, and declining to conteft the principles contained in that work, he fays, " This will moft " probably be done *(if fuch writings fhall be* " *thought to deferve any other refutation than that* " *of criminal juftice)* by others, who may think " with Mr. Burke and with the fame zeal."

In the firft place, it has not yet been done by any body. Not lefs, I believe, than eight or ten pamphlets intended as anfwers to the former part of the " Rights of Man" have been publifhed by different perfons, and not one of them, to my knowledge, has extended to a fecond edition, nor are even the titles of them fo much as generally remembered. As I am averfe to unneceffarily multiplying publications, I have anfwered none of them. And as I believe that a man may write

himfelf

himfelf out of reputation when nobody elfe can do it, I am careful to avoid that rock.

But as I would decline unneceffary publications on the one hand, fo would I avoid every thing that might appear like fullen pride on the other. If Mr. Burke, or any perfon on his fide the queftion, will produce an anfwer to the "Rights of Man," that fhall extend to an half, or even to a fourth part of the number of copies to which the Rights of Man extended, I will reply to his work. But until this be done, I fhall fo far take the fenfe of the public for my guide (and the world knows I am not a flatterer) that what they do not think worth while to read, is not worth mine to anfwer. I fuppofe the number of copies to which the firft part of the *Rights of Man* extended, taking England, Scotland, and Ireland, is not lefs than between forty and fifty thoufand.

I now come to remark on the remaining part of the quotation I have made from Mr. Burke.

"If," fays he, "fuch writings fhall be thought "to deferve any other refutation than that of *cri-* "*minal* juftice."

Pardoning the pun, it muft be *criminal* juftice indeed that fhould condemn a work as a fubftitute for not being able to refute it. The greateft condemnation that could be paffed upon it would be a refutation. But in proceeding by the method Mr. Burke alludes to, the condemnation would, in the final event, pafs upon the criminality of the procefs and not upon the work, and in this cafe, I

had

had rather be the author, than be either the judge, or the jury, that should condemn it.

But to come at once to the point. I have differed from some professional gentlemen on the subject of prosecutions, and I since find they are falling into my opinion, which I will here state as fully, but as concisely as I can.

I will first put a case with respect to any law, and then compare it with a government, or with what in England is, or has been, called a constitution.

It would be an act of despotism, or what in England is called arbitrary power, to make a law to prohibit investigating the principles, good or bad, on which such a law, or any other is founded.

If a law be bad, it is one thing to oppose the practice of it, but it is quite a different thing to expose its errors, to reason on its defects, and to shew cause why it should be repealed, or why another ought to be substituted in its place. I have always held it an opinion (making it also my practice) that it is better to obey a bad law, making use at the same time of every argument to shew its errors and procure its repeal, than forcibly to violate it; because the precedent of breaking a bad law might weaken the force, and lead to a diseretionary violation, of those which are good.

The case is the same with respect to principles and forms of government, or to what are called constitutions and the parts of which they are composed.

It

It is for the good of nations, and not for the emolument or aggrandizement of particular individuals, that government ought to be eſtabliſhed, and that mankind are at the expence of ſupporting it. The defects of every government and conſtitution, both as to principle and form muſt, on a parity of reaſoning, be as open to diſcuſſion as the defects of a law, and it is a duty which every man owes to ſociety to point them out. When thoſe defects, and the means of remedying them are generally ſeen by a nation, that nation will reform its government or its conſtitution in the one caſe, as the government repealed or reformed the law in the other. The operation of government is reſtricted to the making and the adminiſtering of laws; but it is to a nation that the right of forming or reforming, generating or regenerating conſtitutions and governments belong; and conſequently thoſe ſubjects, as ſubjects of inveſtigation, are always before a country *as a matter of right,* and cannot, without invading the general rights of that country, be made ſubjects for proſecution. On this ground I will meet Mr. Burke whenever he pleaſe. It is better that the whole argument ſhould come out, than to ſeek to ſtifle it. It was himſelf that opened the controverſy, and he ought not to deſert it.

I do not believe that monarchy and ariſtocracy will continue ſeven years longer in any of the enlightened countries in Europe. If better reaſons can be ſhewn for them than againſt them, they will ſtand; if the contrary, they will not. Mankind

are

are not now to be told they fhall not think, or they fhall not read; and publications that go no farther than to inveftigate principles of government, to invite men to reafon and to reflect, and to fhew the errors and excellences of different fyftems, have a right to appear. If they do not excite attention, they are not worth the trouble of a profecution; and if they do, the profecution will amount to nothing, fince it cannot amount to a prohibition of reading. This would be a fentence on the public, inftead of the author, and would alfo be the moft effectual mode of making or haftening revolutions.

On all cafes that apply univerfally to a nation, with refpect to fyftems of government, a jury of *twelve* men is not competent to decide. Where there are no witneffes to be examined, no facts to be proved, and where the whole matter is before the whole public, and the merits or demerits of it refting on their opinion; and where there is nothing to be known in a court, but what every body knows out of it, every twelve men is equally as good a jury as the other, and would moft probably reverfe each other's verdict; or from the variety of their opinions, not be able to form one. It is one cafe, whether a nation approve a work, or a plan; but it is quite another cafe, whether it will commit to any fuch jury the power of determining whether that nation have a right to, or fhall reform its government, or not. I mention thofe cafes, that Mr. Burke may fee I have not written on Government without

without reflecting on what is Law, as well as on what are Rights.—The only effectual jury in such cases would be, a convention of the whole nation fairly elected; for in all such cases the whole nation is the vicinage. If Mr. Burke will propose such a jury, I will wave all privileges of being the citizen of another country, and, defending its principles, abide the issue, provided he will do the same; for my opinion is, that his work and his principles would be condemned instead of mine.

As to the prejudices which men have from education and habit, in favour of any particular form or system of government, those prejudices have yet to stand the test of reason and reflection. In fact, such prejudices are nothing. No man is prejudiced in favour of a thing, knowing it to be wrong. He is attached to it on the belief of its being right; and when he see it is not so, the prejudice will be gone. We have but a defective idea of what prejudice is. It might be said, that until men think for themselves the whole is prejudice, and *not opinion*; for that only is opinion which is the result of reason and reflection. I offer this remark, that Mr. Burke may not confide too much in what has been the customary prejudices of the country.

I do not believe that the people of England have ever been fairly and candidly dealt by. They have been imposed upon by parties, and by men assuming the character of leaders. It is time that the nation should rise above those trifles. It is time to dismiss that inattention which has so long been

been the encouraging caufe of ftretching taxation to excefs. It is time to difmifs all thofe
fongs and toafts which are calculated to enflave,
and operate to fuffocate reflection. On all fuch
fubjects men have but to think, and they will neither act wrong nor be mifled. To fay that any
people are not fit for freedom, is to make poverty
their choice, and to fay they had rather be loaded
with taxes than not. If fuch a cafe could be
proved, it would equally prove, that thofe who
govern are not fit to govern them, for they are a
part of the fame national mafs.

But admitting governments to be changed all
over Europe; it certainly may be done without
convulfion or revenge. It is not worth making
changes or revolutions, unlefs it be for fome great
national benefit; and when this fhall appear to a
nation, the danger will be, as in America and
France, to thofe who oppofe; and with this reflection I clofe my Preface.

THOMAS PAINE.

Londdon, Feb. 9, 1792.

CONTENTS.

RIGHTS OF MAN.

PART II.

INTRODUCTION.

WHAT Archimedes faid of the mechanical powers, may be applied, to Reafon and Liberty: " *Had we,*" faid he, " *a place to ftand* " *upon, we might raife the world.*"

The revolution of America prefented in politics what was only theory in mechanics. So deeply rooted were all the governments of the old world, and fo effectually had the tyranny and the antiquity of habit eftablifhed itfelf over the mind, that no beginning could be made in Afia, Africa, or Europe, to reform the political condition of man. Freedom had been hunted round the globe; reafon was confidered as rebellion; and the flavery of fear had made men afraid to think.

But fuch is the irrefiftible nature of truth, that all it afks, and all it wants, is the liberty of appearing. The fun needs no infcfiption to diftinguifh him from darknefs; and no fooner did the American governments difplay themfelves to the world, than

B   defpotifm

defpotifm felt a fhock, and man began to contemplate redrefs.

The independence of America, confidered merely as a feparation from England, would have been
a matter but of little importance, had it not been
accompanied by a revolution in the principles and
practice of governments. She made a ftand, not
for herfelf only, but for the world, and looked
beyond the advantages herfelf could receive. Even
the Heffian, though hired to fight againft her,
may live to blefs his defeat; and England, con-
demning the vicioufnefs of its government, rejoice
in its mifcarriage.

As America was the only fpot in the political
world, where the principles of univerfal reformation could begin, fo alfo was it the beft in the
natural world.   An affemblage of circumftances
confpired, not only to give birth, but to add
gigantic maturity to its principles.   The fcene
which that country prefents to the eye of a fpectator, has fomething in it which generates and
encourages great ideas.   Nature appears to him
in magnitude.   The mighty objects he beholds,
act upon his mind by enlarging it, and he partakes of the greatnefs he contemplates.—Its firft
fettlers were emigrants from different European
nations, and of diverfified profeffions of religion,
retiring from the governmental perfecutions of the
old world, and meeting in the new, not as enemies, but as brothers. The wants which neceffarily
accompany the cultivation of a wildernefs produced
among them a ftate of fociety, which countries,
long haraffed by the quarrels and intrigues of
                              governments,

governments, had neglected to cherifh.   In fuch a fituation man becomes what he ought.   He fees his fpecies, not with the inhuman idea of a natural enemy, but as kindred; and the example fhews to the artificial world, that man muft go back to Nature for information.

From the rapid progrefs which America makes in every fpecies of improvement, it is rational to conclude, that if the governments of Afia, Africa, and Europe, had begun on a principle fimilar to that of America, or had not been very early corrupted therefrom, that thofe countries muft by this time have been in a far fuperior condition to what they are.   Age after age has paffed away, for no other purpofe than to behold their wretchednefs.—Could we fuppofe a fpectator who knew nothing of the world, and who was put into it merely to make his obfervations, he would take a great part of the old world to be new, juft ftruggling with the difficulties and hardfhips of an infant fettlement.   He could not fuppofe that the hordes of miferable poor, with which old countries abound, could be any other than thofe who had not yet had time to provide for themfelves.   Little would he think they were the confequence of what in fuch countries is called government.

If, from the more wretched parts of the old world, we look at thofe which are in an advanced ftage of improvement, we ftill find the greedy hand of government thrufting itfelf into every corner and crevice of induftry, and grafping the fpoil of the multitude.   Invention is continually exercifed, to furnifh new pretences for revenue

and

and taxation.   It watches profperity as its prey, and permits none to efcape without a tribute.

As revolutions have begun, (and as the probability is always greater againft a thing beginning, than of proceeding after it has begun), it is natural to expect that other revolutions will follow.   The amazing and ftill increafing expences with which old governments are conducted, the numerous wars they engage in or provoke, the embarraffments they throw in the way of univerfal civilization and commerce, and the oppreffion and ufurpation they act at home, have wearied out the patience, and exhaufted the property of the world.   In fuch a fituation, and with the examples already exifting, revolutions are to be looked for.   They are become fubjects of univerfal converfation, and may be confidered as the *Order of the day*.

If fyftems of government can be introduced, lefs expenfive, and more productive of general happinefs, than thofe which have exifted, all attempts to oppofe their progrefs will in the end be fruitlefs.   Reafon, like time, will make its own way, and prejudice will fall in a combat with intereft.   If univerfal peace, civilization, and commerce, are ever to be the happy lot of man, it cannot be accomplifhed but by a revolution in the fyftem of governments.   All the monarchical governments are military.   War is their trade, plunder and revenue their objects.   While fuch governments continue, peace has not the abfolute fecurity of a day.   What is the hiftory of all monarchical governments, but a difguftful picture of human wretchednefs, and the accidental refpite

of

of a few years repofe? Wearied with war, and
tired with human butchery, they fat down to reft
and called it peace. This certainly is not the
condition that Heaven intended for man; and if
this be monarchy, well might monarchy be reckoned among the fins of the Jews.

The revolutions which formerly took place in
the world, had nothing in them that interefted the
bulk of mankind. They extended only to a
change of perfons and meafures but not of principles, and rofe or fell among the common tranf-
actions of the moment. What we now behold,
may not improperly be called a " *counter revolution.*" Conqueft and tyranny, at fome early
period, difpoffeffed man of his rights, and he is
now recovering them. And as the tide of all human affairs has its ebb and flow in directions contrary to each other, fo alfo is it in this. Government founded on a *moral theory, on a fyftem of
univerfal peace, on the indefeafible hereditary Rights
of Man*, is now revolving from weft to eaft, by a
ftronger impulfe than the government of the
fword revolved from eaft to weft. It interefts not
particular individuals, but nations, in its progrefs,
and promifes a new æra to the human race.

The danger to which the fuccefs of revolutions
is moft expofed, is that of attempting them before
the principles on which they proceed, and the
advantages to refult from them, are fufficiently
feen and underftood. Almoft every thing appertaining to the circumftances of a nation, has been
abforbed and confounded under the general and

myfterious

myfterious word *government*. Though it avoids taking to its account the errors it commits, and the mifchiefs it occafions, it fails not to arrogate to itfelf whatever has the appearance of profperity. It robs induftry of its honours, by pedanticly making itfelf the caufe of its effects; and purloins from the general character of man, the merits that appertain to him as a focial being.

It may therefore be of ufe, in this day of revolutions, to difcriminate between thofe things which are the effect of government, and thofe which are not. This will beft be done by taking a review of fociety and civilization, and the confequences refulting therefrom, as things diftinct from what are called governments. By beginning with this inveftigation, we fhall be able to affign effects to their proper caufe, and analize the mafs of common errors.

1   CHAP. I.

CHAP. I.

Of SOCIETY AND CIVILIZATION.

GREAT part of that order which reigns among mankind is not the effect of government. It has its origin in the principles of fociety and the natural conftitution of man. It exifted prior to government, and would exift if the formality of government was abolifhed. The mutual dependance and reciprocal intereft which man has upon man, and all the parts of a civilized community upon each other, create that great chain of connection which holds it together. The landholder, the farmer, the manufacturer, the merchant, the tradefman, and every occupation, profpers by the aid which each receives from the other, and from the whole. Common intereft regulates their concerns, and forms their law; and the laws which common ufage ordains, have a greater influence than the laws of government. In fine, fociety performs for itfelf almoft every thing which is afcribed to government.

To underftand the nature and quantity of government proper for man, it is neceffary to attend to his character. As Nature created him

for focial life, fhe fitted him for the ftation fhe
intended. In all cafes fhe made his natural wants
greater than his individual powers. No one man
is capable, without the aid of fociety, of fupplying
his own wants; and thofe wants, acting upon every
individual, impel the whole of them into fociety,
as naturally as gravitation acts to a center.

But fhe has gone further. She has not only
forced man into fociety, by a diverfity of wants,
which the reciprocal aid of each other can fupply,
but fhe has implanted in him a fyftem of focial
affections, which, though not neceffary to his exiftence, are effential to his happinefs. There is no
period in life when this love for fociety ceafes to
act. It begins and ends with our being.

If we examine, with attention, into the compo-
fition and conftitution of man, the diverfity of
his wants, and the diverfity of talents in different men for reciprocally accommodating the
wants of each other, his propenfity to fociety, and
confequently to preferve the advantages refulting
from it, we fhall eafily difcover, that a great part
of what is called government is mere impofition.

Government is no farther neceffary than to fupply
the few cafes to which fociety and civilization are
not conveniently competent; and inftances are not
wanting to fhew, that every thing which government can ufefully add thereto, has been performed by the common confent of fociety, without
government.

For upwards of two years from the commencement of the American war, and to a longer period

in

in several of the American States, there were no established forms of government. The old governments had been abolished, and the country was too much occupied in defence, to employ its attention in establishing new governments; yet during this interval, order and harmony were preserved as inviolate as in any country in Europe. There is a natural aptness in man, and more so in society, because it embraces a greater variety of abilities and resource, to accommodate itself to whatever situation it is in. The instant formal government is abolished, society begins to act. A general association takes place, and common interest produces common security.

So far is it from being true, as has been pretended, that the abolition of any formal government is the dissolution of society, that it acts by a contrary impulse, and brings the latter the closer together. All that part of its organization which it had committed to its government, devolves again upon itself, and acts through its medium. When men, as well from natural instinct, as from reciprocal benefits, have habituated themselves to social and civilized life, there is always enough of its principles in practice to carry them through any changes they may find necessary or convenient to make in their government. In short, man is so naturally a creature of society, that it is almost impossible to put him out of it.

Formal government makes but a small part of civilized life; and when even the best that human
wisdom

wifdom can devife is eftablifhed, it is a thing
more in name and idea, than in fact. It is to
the great and fundamental principles of fociety
and civilization—to the common ufage univerfally
confented to, and mutually and reciprocally maintained—to the unceafing circulation of intereft,
which, paffing through its million channels, in-
vigorates the whole mafs of civilized man—it is
to thefe things, infinitely more than to any thing
which even the beft inftituted government can
perform, that the fafety and profperity of the
individual and of the whole depends.

The more perfect civilization is, the lefs occafion
has it for government, becaufe the more does it
regulate its own affairs, and govern itfelf; but fo
contrary is the practice of old governments to the
reafon of the cafe, that the expences of them increafe in the proportion they ought to diminifh.
It is but few general laws that civilized life requires, and thofe of fuch common ufefulnefs,
that whether they are enforced by the forms of
government or not, the effect will be nearly the
fame.   If we confider what the principles are
that firft condenfe men into fociety, and what the
motives that regulate their mutual intercourfe
afterwards, we fhall find, by the time we arrive at
what is called government, that nearly the whole
of the bufinefs is performed by the natural operation of the parts upon each other.

Man, with refpect to all thofe matters, is more
a creature of confiftency than he is aware, or that
governments

governments would wifh him to believe. All the great laws of fociety are laws of nature. Thofe of trade and commerce, whether with refpect to the intercourfe of individuals, or of nations, are laws of mutual and reciprocal intereft. They are followed and obeyed, becaufe it is the intereft of the parties fo to do, and not on account of any formal laws their governments may impofe or interpofe.

But how often is the natural propenfity to fociety difturbed or deftroyed by the operations of government! When the latter, inftead of being ingrafted on the principles of the former, affumes to exift for itfelf, and acts by partialities of favour and oppreffion, it becomes the caufe of the mifchiefs it ought to prevent.

If we look back to the riots and tumults, which at various times have happened in England, we fhall find, that they did not proceed from the want of a government, but that government was itfelf the generating caufe; inftead of confolidating fociety it divided it; it deprived it of its natural cohefion, and engendered difcontents and diforders, which otherwife would not have exifted. In thofe affociations which men promifcuoufly form for the purpofe of trade, or of any concern, in which government is totally out of the queftion, and in which they act merely on the principles of fociety, we fee how naturally the various parties unite; and this fhews, by comparifon, that governments, fo far from being always the caufe or means of order, are often the
deftruction

destruction of it. The riots of 1780 had no other source than the remains of those prejudices, which the government itself had encouraged. But with respect to England there are also other causes.

Excess and inequality of taxation, however disguised in the means, never fail to appear in their effects. As a great mass of the community are thrown thereby into poverty and discontent, they are constantly on the brink of commotion ; and, deprived, as they unfortunately are, of the means of information, are easily heated to outrage. Whatever the apparent cause of any riots may be, the real one is always want of happiness. It shews that something is wrong in the system of government, that injures the felicity by which society is to be preserved.

But as fact is superior to reasoning, the instance of America presents itself to confirm these observations.—If there is a country in the world, where concord, according to common calculation, would be least expected, it is America. Made up, as it is, of people from different nations *, accustomed

to

* That part of America which is generally called New-England, including New-Hampshire, Massachusetts, Rhode-Island, and Connecticut, is peopled chiefly by English descendants. In the state of New-York, about half are Dutch, the rest English, Scotch, and Irish. In New-Jersey, a mixture of English and Dutch, with some Scotch and Irish. In Pennsylvania, about one third are English, another Germans, and the remainder Scotch and Irish, with some Swedes. The States to the southward have a greater proportion of English than the middle States, but in all of them there is a mixture ; and besides those enumerated,

to different forms and habits of government, speaking different languages, and more different in their modes of worſhip, it would appear that the union of ſuch a people was impracticable; but by the ſimple operation of conſtructing government on the principles of ſociety and the rights of man, every difficulty retires, and all the parts are brought into cordial uniſon. There, the poor are not oppreſſed, the rich are not privileged. Induſtry is not mortified by the ſplendid extravagance of a court rioting at its expence. Their taxes are few, becauſe their government is juſt; and as there is nothing to render them wretched, there is nothing to engender riots and tumults.

A metaphyſical man, like Mr. Burke, would have tortured his invention to diſcover how ſuch a people could be governed. He would have ſuppoſed that ſome muſt be managed by fraud, others by force, and all by ſome contrivance; that genius muſt be hired to impoſe upon ignorance, and ſhew and parade to faſcinate the vulgar. Loſt in the abundance of his reſearches, he would have reſolved and re-reſolved, and finally overlooked the plain and eaſy road that lay directly before him.

One of the great advantages of the American revolution has been, that it led to a diſcovery of

enumerated, there are a conſiderable number of French, and ſome few of all the European nations lying on the coaſt. The moſt numerous religious denomination are the Preſbyterians; but no one ſect is eſtabliſhed above another, and all men are equally citizens.

the

the principles, and laid open the impofition of governments.   All the revolutions till then had been
worked within the atmofphere of a court, and
never on the great floor of a nation.   The parties
were always of the clafs of courtiers; and whatever was their rage for reformation, they carefully
preferved the fraud of the profeffion.

In all cafes they took care to reprefent government as a thing made up of myfteries, which only
themfelves underftood ; and they hid from the
underftanding of the nation, the only thing that
was beneficial to know, namely, *That government is nothing more than a national affociation
acting on the principles of fociety.*

HAVING thus endeavoured to fhew, that the
focial and civilized ftate of man is capable of
performing within itfelf, almoft every thing
neceffary to its protection and government, it
will be proper, on the other hand, to take a
review of the prefent old governments, and
examine whether their principles and practice are
correfpondent thereto.

CHAP. II.

CHAP. II.

Of the ORIGIN of the PRESENT OLD GOVERNMENTS.

IT is impoſſible that ſuch governments as have hitherto exiſted in the world, could have commenced by any other means than a total violation of every principle ſacred and moral. The obſcurity in which the origin of all the preſent old governments is buried, implies the iniquity and diſgrace with which they began. The origin of the preſent government of America and France will ever be remembered, becauſe it is honourable to record it ; but with reſpect to the reſt, even Flattery has conſigned them to the tomb of time, without an inſcription.

It could have been no difficult thing in the early and ſolitary ages of the world, while the chief employment of men was that of attending flocks and herds, for a banditti of ruffians to overrun a country, and lay it under contributions. Their power being thus eſtabliſhed, the chief of the band contrived to loſe the name of Robber in that of Monarch; and hence the origin of Monarchy and Kings.

The

The origin of the government of England, fo far as relates to what is called its line of monarchy, being one of the lateſt, is perhaps the beſt recorded. The hatred which the Norman invaſion and tyranny begat, muſt have been deeply rooted in the nation, to have outlived the contrivance to obliterate it. Though not a courtier will talk of the curfeu bell, not a village in England has forgotten it.

Thoſe bands of robbers having parcelled out the world, and divided it into dominions, began, as is naturally the caſe, to quarrel with each other. What at firſt was obtained by violence, was conſidered by others as lawful to be taken, and a ſecond plunderer ſucceeded the firſt. They alternately invaded the dominions which each had aſſigned to himſelf, and the brutality with which they treated each other explains the original character of monarchy. It was ruffian torturing ruffian. The conqueror conſidered the conquered, not as his priſoner, but his property. He led him in triumph rattling in chains, and doomed him, at pleaſure, to ſlavery or death. As time obliterated the hiſtory of their beginning, their ſucceſſors aſſumed new appearances, to cut off the entail of their diſgrace, but their principles and objects remained the ſame. What at firſt was plunder, aſſumed the ſofter name of revenue; and the power originally uſurped, they affected to inherit.

From ſuch beginning of governments, what could be expected, but a continual ſyſtem of war and extortion? It has eſtabliſhed itſelf into a trade. The vice is not peculiar to one more than

to

to another, but is the common principle of all.
There does not exiſt within ſuch governments, a
ſtamina whereon to ingraft reformation; and the
ſhorteſt and moſt effectual remedy is to begin
anew.

What ſcenes of horror, what perfection of ini‐
quity, preſent themſelves in contemplating the
character, and reviewing the hiſtory of ſuch go‐
vernments! If we would delineate human nature
with a baſeneſs of heart, and hypocriſy of coun‐
tenance, that reflection would ſhudder at and hu‐
manity diſown, it is kings, courts, and cabinets,
that muſt ſit for the portrait. Man, naturally as
he is, with all his faults about him, is not up to
the character.

Can we poſſibly ſuppoſe that if governments
had originated in a right principle, and had not
an intereſt in purſuing a wrong one, that the
world could have been in the wretched and quar‐
relſome condition we have ſeen it? What induce‐
ment has the farmer, while following the plough,
to lay aſide his peaceful purſuits, and go to war
with the farmer of another country? or what
inducement has the manufacturer? What is
dominion to them, or to any claſs of men in a
nation? Does it add an acre to any man's
eſtate, or raiſe its value? Are not conqueſt and
defeat each of the ſame price, and taxes the never‐
failing conſequence?—Though this reaſoning may
be good to a nation, it is not ſo to a government.
War is the Pharo table of governments, and na‐
tions the dupes of the game.

C

If there is any thing to wonder at in this miſerable ſcene of governments, more than might be expeded, it is the progreſs which the peaceful arts of agriculture, manufaĉture and commerce have made, beneath ſuch a long accumulating load of diſcouragement and oppreſſion.   It ſerves to ſhew, that inſtinĉt in animals does not aĉt with ſtronger impulſe, than the principles of ſociety and civilization operate in man. Under all diſcouragements, he purſues his objeĉt, and yields to nothing but impoſſibilities.

C H A P. III.

CHAP. III.

OF THE OLD AND NEW SYSTEMS OF GOVERNMENT.

NOTHING can appear more contradictory than the principles on which the old governments began, and the condition to which fociety, civilization, and commerce, are capable of carrying mankind. Government on the old fyftem, is an affumption of power, for the aggrandifement of itfelf; on the new, a delegation of power, for the common benefit of fociety. The former fupports itfelf by keeping up a fyftem of war; the latter promotes a fyftem of peace, as the true means of enriching a nation. The one encourages national prejudices; the other promotes univerfal fociety, as the means of univerfal commerce. The one meafures its profperity, by the quantity of revenue it extorts; the other proves its excellence, by the fmall quantity of taxes it requires.

Mr. Burke has talked of old and new whigs. If he can amufe himfelf with childifh names and diftinctions, I fhall not interrupt his pleafure. It is not to him, but to the Abbé Sieyes, that I addrefs this chapter. I am already engaged to

the

the latter gentleman, to difcufs the fubject of
monarchical government; and as it naturally
occurs in comparing the old and new fyftems,
I make this the opportunity of prefenting to
him my obfervations.   I fhall occafionally take
Mr. Burke in my way.

Though it might be proved that the fyftem of
government now called the NEW, is the moft ancient
in principle of all that have exifted, being founded
on the original inherent Rights of Man: yet, as
tyranny and the fword have fufpended the exercife
of thofe rights for many centuries paft, it ferves
better the purpofe of diftinction to call it the *new*,
than to claim the right of calling it the old.

The firft general diftinction between thofe two
fyftems, is, that the one now called the old is
hereditary, either in whole or in part; and the
new is entirely *reprefentative*.   It rejects all hereditary government:

Firft, As being an impofition on mankind.

Secondly, As inadequate to the purpofes for
which government is neceffary.

With refpect to the firft of thefe heads—It cannot be proved by what right hereditary government could begin: neither does there exift within
the compafs of mortal power, a right to eftablifh
it.   Man has no authority over pofterity in
matters of perfonal right; and therefore, no man,
or body of men, had, or can have, a right to fet
up hereditary government.   Were even ourfelves to come again into exiftence, inftead of
being fucceeded by pofterity, we have not now
the right of taking from ourfelves the rights

2   which

which would then be ours. On what ground, then, do we pretend to take them from others?

All hereditary government is in its nature tyranny. An heritable crown, or an heritable throne, or by what other fanciful name such things may be called, have no other significant explanation than that mankind are heritable property. To inherit a government, is to inherit the people, as if they were flocks and herds.

With respect to the second head, that of being inadequate to the purposes for which government is necessary, we have only to consider what government essentially is, and compare it with the circumstances to which hereditary succession is subject.

Government ought to be a thing always in full maturity. It ought to be so constructed as to be superior to all the accidents to which individual man is subject; and therefore, hereditary succession, by being *subject to them all*, is the most irregular and imperfect of all the systems of government.

We have heard the *Rights of Man* called a *levelling* system; but the only system to which the word *levelling* is truly applicable, is the hereditary monarchical system. It is a system of *mental levelling*. It indiscriminately admits every species of character to the same authority. Vice and virtue, ignorance and wisdom, in short, every quality, good or bad, is put on the same level Kings succeed each other, not as rationals, but as animals. It signifies not what their mental or moral characters are. Can we then be surprised

C 3   at

at the abject state of the human mind in monarchical countries, when the government itself is
formed on such an abject levelling system ?—It
has no fixed character.   To day it is one thing;
to-morrow it is something else.   It changes with
the temper of every succeeding individual, and
is subject to all the varieties of each.   It is government through the medium of passions and accidents.   It appears under all the various characters of childhood, decrepitude, dotage, a thing
at nurse, in leading-strings, or in crutches.   It
reverses the wholesome order of nature.   It occasionally puts children over men, and the conceits
of non-age over wisdom and experience.   In short,
we cannot conceive a more ridiculous figure of
government, than hereditary succession, in all its
cases, presents.

Could it be made a decree in nature, or an
edict registered in heaven, and man could know
it, that virtue and wisdom should invariably appertain to hereditary succession, the objections to it
would be removed ; but when we see that nature
acts as if she disowned and sported with the hereditary system ; that the mental characters of
successors, in all countries, are below the average
of human understanding ; that one is a tyrant,
another an ideot, a third insane, and some all
three together, it is impossible to attach confi-
dence to it, when reason in man has power to
act.

It is not to the Abbé Sieyes that I need apply this
reasoning ; he has already saved me that trouble,
by giving his own opinion upon the case.   " If it
                                                " be

" be afked," fays he, "what is my opinion with
" refpect to hereditary right, I anfwer, without
" hefitation, That, in good theory, an hereditary
" tranfmiffion of any power or office, can never
" accord with the laws of a true reprefentation.
" Hereditaryfhip is, in this fenfe, as much an
" attaint upon principle, as an outrage upon fo-
" ciety. But let us," continues he, " refer to the
" hiftory of all elective monarchies and principali-
" ties : Is there one in which the elective mode is
" not worfe than the hereditary fucceffion ?"

As to debating on which is the worft of the two,
is admitting both to be bad ; and herein we are
agreed. The preference which the Abbé has given,
is a condemnation of the thing that he prefers. Such
a mode of reafoning on fuch a fubject is inadmiffible,
becaufe it finally amounts to an accufation upon
Providence, as if fhe had left to man no other
choice with refpect to government than between
two evils, the beft of which he admits to be
" *an attaint upon principle, and an outrage upon
fociety.*"

Paffing over, for the prefent, all the evils and
mifchiefs which monarchy has occafioned in the
world, nothing can more effectually prove its ufe-
lefsnefs in a ftate of *civil government*, than making
it hereditary. Would we make any office hereditary that required wifdom and abilities to fill
it ? and where wifdom and abilities are not neceffary, fuch an office, whatever it may be, is
fuperfluous or infignificant.

Hereditary fucceffion is a burlefque upon
monarchy. It puts it in the moft ridiculous

C 4   light,

light, by prefenting it as an office which any
child or ideot may fill. It requires fome talents
to be a common mechanic; but, to be a king,
requires only the animal figure of man—a fort
of breathing automaton. This fort of fuperftition
may laft a few years more, but it cannot long
refift the awakened reafon and intereft of man.

As to Mr. Burke, he is a ftickler for monarchy,
not altogether as a penfioner, if he is one, which I
believe, but as a political man. He has taken
up a contemptible opinion of mankind, who, in
their turn, are taking up the fame of him. He
confiders them as a herd of beings that muft be
governed by fraud, effigy and fhew; and an idol
would be as good a figure of monarchy with
him, as a man. I will, however, do him the
juftice to fay, that, with refpect to America, he
has been very complimentary. He always con-
tended, at leaft in my hearing, that the people of
America were more enlightened than thofe of
England, or of any country in Europe; and that
therefore the impofition of fhew was not neceffary in their governments.

Though the comparifon between hereditary and
elective monarchy, which the Abbe has made, is
unneceffary to the cafe, becaufe the reprefentative
fyftem rejects both; yet, were I to make the comparifon, I fhould decide contrary to what he has
done.

The civil wars which have originated from con-
tefted hereditary claims, are more numerous, and
have been more dreadful, and of longer continu-
ance, than thofe which have been occafioned by
election.

election. All the civil wars in France arofe from the hereditary fyftem; they were either produced by hereditary claims, or by the imperfection of the hereditary form, which admits of regencies, or monarchy at nurfe. With refpect to England, its hiftory is full of the fame misfortunes. The contefts for fucceffion between the Houfes of York and Lancafter, lafted a whole century; and others of a fimilar nature, have renewed themfelves fince that period. Thofe of 1715 and 1745, were of the fame kind. The fucceffion war for the crown of Spain, embroiled almoft half Europe. The difturbances in Holland are generated from the hereditaryfhip of the Stadtholder. A government calling itfelf free, with an hereditary office, is like a thorn in the flefh, that produces a fermentation which endeavours to difcharge it.

But I might go further, and place alfo foreign wars, of whatever kind, to the fame caufe. It is by adding the evil of hereditary fucceffion to that of monarchy, that a permanent family-intereft is created, whofe conftant objects are dominion and revenue. Poland, though an elective monarchy, has had fewer wars than thofe which are hereditary; and it is the only government that has made a voluntary effay, though but a fmall one, to reform the condition of the country.

Having thus glanced at a few of the defects of the old, or hereditary fyftems of government, let us compare it with the new, or reprefentative fyftem.

The reprefentative fyftem takes fociety and civilization for its bafis; nature, reafon, and experience, for its guide.

Experience,

Experience, in all ages, and in all countries, has demonſtrated, that it is impoſſible to controul Nature in her diſtribution of mental powers. She gives them as ſhe pleaſes. Whatever is the rule by which ſhe, apparently to us, ſcatters them among mankind, that rule remains a ſecret to man. It would be as ridiculous to attempt to fix the hereditaryſhip of human beauty, as of wiſdom. Whatever wiſdom conſtituently is, it is like a ſeedleſs plant; it may be reared when it appears, but it cannot be voluntarily produced. There is always a ſufficiency ſomewhere in the general maſs of ſociety for all purpoſes; but with reſpect to the parts of ſociety, it is continually changing its place. It riſes in one to-day, in another to-morrow, and has moſt probably viſited in rotation every family of the earth, and again withdrawn.

As this is the order of nature, the order of government muſt neceſſarily follow it, or government will, as we ſee it does, degenerate into ignorance. The hereditary ſyſtem, therefore, is as repugnant to human wiſdom, as to human rights; and is as abſurd, as it is unjuſt.

As the republic of letters brings forward the beſt literary productions, by giving to genius a fair and univerſal chance; ſo the repreſentative ſyſtem of government is calculated to produce the wiſeſt laws, by collecting wiſdom from where it can be found. I ſmile to myſelf when I contemplate the ridiculous inſignificance into which literature and all the ſciences would ſink, were they made hereditary; and I carry the ſame idea into governments. An hereditary governor is as inconſiſtent as an

hereditary

hereditary author. I know not whether Homer or Euclid had fons: but I will venture an opinion, that if they had, and had left their works unfinifhed, thofe fons could not have completed them.

Do we need a ftronger evidence of the abfurdity of hereditary government, than is feen in the defcendants of thofe men, in any line of life, who once were famous? Is there fcarcely an inftance in which there is not a total reverfe of the character? It appears as if the tide of mental faculties flowed as far as it could in certain channels, and then forfook its courfe, and arofe in others. How irrational then is the hereditary fyftem which eftablifhes channels of power, in company with which wifdom refufes to flow! By continuing this abfurdity, man is perpetually in contradiction with himfelf; he accepts, for a king, or a chief magiftrate, or a legiflator, a perfon whom he would not elect for a conftable.

It appears to general obfervation, that revolutions create genius and talents; but thofe events do no more than bring them forward. There is exifting in man, a mafs of fenfe lying in a dormant ftate, and which, unlefs fomething excites it to action, will defcend with him, in that condition, to the grave. As it is to the advantage of fociety that the whole of its faculties fhould be employed, the conftruction of government ought to be fuch as to bring forward, by a quiet and regular operation, all that extent of capacity which never fails to appear in revolutions.

This cannot take place in the infipid ftate of

hereditary

hereditary government, not only becaufe it pre-
vents, but becaufe it operates to benumb. When
the mind of a nation is bowed down by any political fuperftition in its government, fuch as hereditary fucceffion is, it lofes a confiderable portion
of its powers on all other fubjects and objects.
Hereditary fucceffion requires the fame obedience to ignorance, as to wifdom; and when once
the mind can bring itfelf to pay this indifcrimi-
nate reverence, it defcends below the ftature of
mental manhood. It is fit to be great only in
little things. It acts a treachery upon itfelf,
and fuffocates the fenfations that urge to de-
tection.

Though the ancient governments prefent to us
a miferable picture of the condition of man, there
is one which above all others exempts itfelf from
the general defcription. I mean the democracy
of the Athenians. We fee more to admire, and
lefs to condemn, in that great, extraordinary people, than in any thing which hiftory affords.

Mr. Burke is fo little acquainted with confti-
tuent principles of government, that he confounds
democracy and reprefentation together. Reprefentation was a thing unknown in the ancient democracies. In thofe the mafs of the people met
and enacted laws (grammatically fpeaking) in
the firft perfon. Simple democracy was no other
than the common-hall of the ancients. It fignifies the *form*, as well as the public principle of the
government. As thefe democracies increafed in
population, and the territory extended, the fimple
democratical

democratical form became unwieldy and impracticable; and as the fyftem of reprefentation was
not known, the confequence was, they either
degenerated convulfively into monarchies, or became abforbed into fuch as then exifted. Had
the fyftem of reprefentation been then underftood, as it now is, there is no reafon to believe
that thofe forms of government, now called monarchical or ariftocratical, would ever have taken
place. It was the want of fome method to
confolidate the parts of fociety, after it became
too populous, and too extenfive for the fimple
democratical form, and alfo the lax and fo-
litary condition of fhepherds and herdfmen in
other parts of the world, that afforded opportunities to thofe unnatural modes of government
to begin.

As it is neceffary to clear away the rubbifh of
errors, into which the fubject of government has
been thrown, I fhall proceed to remark on fome
others.

It has always been the political craft of courtiers and court-governments, to abufe fomething
which they called republicanifm; but what republicanifm was, or is, they never attempt to explain.
Let us examine a little into this cafe.

The only forms of government are, the democratical, the ariftocratical, the monarchical, and
what is now called the reprefentative.

What is called a *republic*, is not any *particular
form* of government. It is wholly characteriftical
of the purport, matter, or object for which government ought to be inftituted, and on which
it

it is to be employed, RES-PUBLICA, the public affairs, or the public good; or, literally tranflated, the *public thing*. It is a word of a good original, referring to what ought to be the character and bufinefs of government; and in this fenfe it is naturally oppofed to the word *monarchy*, which has a bafe original fignification. It means arbitrary power in an individual perfon; in the exercife of which, *himfelf*, and not the *res-publica*, is the object.

Every government that does not act on the principle of a *Republic*, or in other words, that does not make the *res-publica* its whole and fole object, is not a good government. Republican government is no other than government eftablifhed and conducted for the intereft of the public, as well individually as collectively. It is not neceffarily connected with any particular form, but it moft naturally affociates with the reprefentative form, as being beft calculated to fecure the end for which a nation is at the expence of fupporting it.

Various forms of government have affected to ftyle themfelves a republic. Poland calls itfelf a republic, which is an hereditary ariftocracy, with what is called an elective monarchy. Holland calls itfelf a republic, which is chiefly ariftocratical, with an hereditary ftadtholderfhip. But the government of America, which is wholly on the fyftem of reprefentation, is the only real republic in character and in practice, that now exifts. Its government has no other object than the public bufinefs of the nation, and therefore it is properly a republic;

a republic; and the Americans have taken care that THIS, and no other, shall always be the object of their government, by their rejecting every thing hereditary, and establishing government on the system of representation only.

Those who have said that a republic is not a *form* of government calculated for countries of great extent, mistook, in the first place, the *business* of a government, for a *form* of government; for the *res-publica* equally appertains to every extent of territory and population. And, in the second place, if they meant any thing with respect to *form*, it was the simple democratical form, such as was the mode of government in the ancient democracies, in which there was no representation. The case, therefore, is not, that a republic cannot be extensive, but that it cannot be extensive on the simple democratical form; and the question naturally presents itself, *What is the best form of government for conducting the* RES-PUBLICA, *or the* PUBLIC BUSINESS *of a nation, after it becomes too extensive and populous for the simple democratical form?*

It cannot be monarchy, because monarchy is subject to an objection of the same amount to which the simple democratical form was subject.

It is possible that an individual may lay down a system of principles, on which government shall be constitutionally established to any extent of territory. This is no more than an operation of the mind, acting by its own powers. But the practice upon those principles, as applying to the
various

various and numerous circumftances of a nation, its agriculture, manufacture, trade, commerce, &c. &c. requires a knowledge of a different kind, and which can be had only from the various parts of fociety. It is an affemblage of practical knowledge, which no one individual can poffefs; and therefore the monarchical form is as much limited, in ufeful practice, from the incompetency of knowledge, as was the democratical form, from the multiplicity of population. The one degenerates, by extenfion, into confufion; the other, into ignorance and incapacity, of which all the great monarchies are an evidence. The monarchical form, therefore, could not be a fubftitute for the democratical, becaufe it has equal inconveniences.

Much lefs could it when made hereditary. This is the moft effectual of all forms to preclude knowledge. Neither could the high democratical mind have voluntarily yielded itfelf to be governed by children and idiots, and all the motley infignificance of character, which attends fuch a mere animal-fyftem, the difgrace and the reproach of reafon and of man.

As to the ariftocratical form, it has the fame vices and defects with the monarchical, except that the chance of abilities is better from the proportion of numbers, but there is ftill no fecurity for the right ufe and application of them*.

Referring, then, to the original fimple democracy,

* For a character of ariftocracy, the reader is referred to *Rights of Man*, Part I. page 70.

it

it affords the true data from which government on a large fcale can begin.   It is incapable of extenfion, not from its principle, but from the inconvenience of its form; and monarchy and ariftocracy, from their incapacity.   Retaining, then, democracy as the ground, and rejecting the corrupt fyftems of monarchy and ariftocracy, the reprefentative fyftem naturally prefents itfelf; remedying at once the defects of the fimple democracy as to form, and the incapacity of the other two with refpect to knowledge.

Simple democracy was fociety governing itfelf without the aid of fecondary means.   By ingrafting reprefentation upon democracy, we arrive at a fyftem of government capable of embracing and confederating all the various interefts and every extent of territory and population; and that alfo with advantages as much fuperior to hereditary government, as the republic of letters is to hereditary literature.

It is on this fyftem that the American government is founded.   It is reprefentation ingrafted upon democracy.   It has fixed the form by a fcale parallel in all cafes to the extent of the principle. What Athens was in miniature, America will be in magnitude.   The one was the wonder of the ancient world; the other is becoming the admiration and model of the prefent.   It is the eafieft of all the forms of government to be underftood, and the moft eligible in practice; and excludes at once the ignorance and infecurity of the hereditary mode, and the inconvenience of the fimple democracy.

It

It is impoſſible to conceive a ſyſtem of government capable of acting over ſuch an extent of
territory, and ſuch a circle of intereſts, as is immediately produced by the operation of repreſentation. France, great and populous as it is, is
but a ſpot in the capacioufneſs of the ſyſtem. It
adapts itſelf to all poſſible caſes. It is preferable
to ſimple democracy even in ſmall territories.
Athens, by repreſentation, would have outrivalled
her own democracy.

That which is called government, or rather
that which we ought to conceive government to
be, is no more than ſome common center, in
which all the parts of ſociety unite. This cannot
be accompliſhed by any method ſo conducive to the
various intereſts of the community, as by the repreſentative ſyſtem. It concentrates the knowledge
neceſſary to the intereſt of the parts, and of the
whole. It places government in a ſtate of
conſtant maturity. It is, as has been already
obſerved, never young, never old. It is ſubject
neither to nonage, nor dotage. It is never in the
cradle, nor on crutches. It admits not of a ſeparation between knowledge and power, and is ſuperior, as government always ought to be, to all
the accidents of individual man, and is therefore
ſuperior to what is called monarchy.

A nation is not a body, the figure of which is
to be repreſented by the human body ; but is like
a body contained within a circle, having a common center, in which every radius meets ; and that
center is formed by repreſentation. To connect
repre-

reprefentation with what is called monarchy, is eccentric government.   Reprefentation is of itfelf the delegated monarchy of a nation, and cannot debafe itfelf by dividing it with another.

Mr. Burke has two or three times, in his parliamentary fpeeches, and in his publications, made ufe of a jingle of words that convey no ideas. Speaking of government, he fays, " It is better " to have monarchy for its bafis, and republican- " ifm for its corrective, than republicanifm for its " bafis, and monarchy for its corrective."—If he means that it is better to correct folly with wifdom, than wifdom with folly, I will no otherwife contend with him, than that it would be much better to reject the folly entirely.

But what is this thing which Mr. Burke calls monarchy? Will he explain it? All men can underftand what reprefentation is ; and that it muft necefarily include a variety of knowledge and talents. But, what fecurity is there for the fame qualities on the part of monarchy? or, when this monarchy is a child, where then is the wifdom? What does it know about government? Who then is the monarch, or where is the monarchy? If it is to be performed by regency, it proves it to be a farce. A regency is a mock fpecies of republic, and the whole of monarchy deferves no better defcription. It is a thing as various as imagination can paint. It has none of the ftable character that government ought to poffefs.   Every fucceffion is a revolution, and every regency a counter revolution.   The whole of it is a fcene of perpetual court

D 2   cabal

cabal and intrigue, of which Mr. Burke is himſelf an inſtance. To render monarchy conſiſtent with government, the next in ſucceſſion ſhould not be born a child, but a man at once, and that man a Solomon. It is ridiculous that nations are to wait, and government be interrupted, till boys grow to be men.

Whether I have too little ſenſe to ſee, or too much to be impoſed upon; whether I have too much or too little pride, or of any thing elſe, I leave out of the queſtion; but certain it is, that what is called monarchy, always appears to me a ſilly, contemptible thing. I compare it to ſome-thing kept behind a curtain, about which there is a great deal of buſtle and fuſs, and a wonderful air of ſeeming ſolemnity; but when, by any acci-dent, the curtain happens to be open, and the company ſee what it is, they burſt into laughter.

In the repreſentative ſyſtem of government, nothing of this can happen. Like the nation itſelf, it poſſeſſes a perpetual ſtamina, as well of body as of mind, and preſents itſelf on the open theatre of the world in a fair and manly manner. Whatever are its excellences or its defects, they are viſible to all. It exiſts not by fraud and myſtery; it deals not in cant and ſophiſtry; but inſpires a language, that, paſſing from heart to heart, is felt and underſtood.

We muſt ſhut our eyes againſt reaſon, we muſt baſely degrade our underſtanding, not to ſee the folly of what is called monarchy. Nature is orderly in all her works; but this is a mode of

govern-

government that counteracts nature.   It turns the
the progrefs of the human faculties upfide down.
It fubjects age to be governed by children, and
wifdom by folly.

On the contrary, the reprefentative fyftem is
always parallel with the order and immutable laws
of nature, and meets the reafon of man in every
part. For example:

In the American federal government, more
power is delegated to the Prefident of the United
States, than to any other individual member of
congrefs. He cannot, therefore, be elected to this
office under the age of thirty-five years. By this
time the judgment of man becomes matured, and
he has lived long enough to be acquainted with
men and things, and the country with him.—But
on the monarchical plan, (exclufive of the numerous chances there are againft every man born into
the world, of drawing a prize in the lottery of human faculties), the next in fucceffion, whatever he
may be, is put at the head of a nation, and of a
government, at the age of eighteen years. Does
this appear like an act of wifdom? Is it confiftent
with the proper dignity and the manly character of
a nation? Where is the propriety of calling fuch
a lad the father of the people?—In all other cafes,
a perfon is a minor until the age of twenty-one
years. Before this period, he is not trufted with
the management of an acre of land, or with the
heritable property of a flock of fheep, or an herd
of fwine; but, wonderful to tell! he may, at the
age of eighteen years, be trufted with a nation.

That monarchy is all a bubble, a mere court artifice to procure money, is evident, (at leaft to me), in every character in which it can be viewed. It would be impoffible, on the rational fyftem of reprefentative government, to make out a bill of expences to fuch an enormous amount as this deception admits. Government is not of itfelf a very chargeable inftitution. The whole expence of the federal government of America, founded, as I have already faid, on the fyftem of reprefentation, and extending over a country nearly ten times as large as England, is but fix hundred thoufand dollars, or one hundred and thirty-five thoufand pounds fterling.

I prefume, that no man in his fober fenfes, will compare the character of any of the kings of Europe with that of General Wafhington. Yet, in France, and alfo in England, the expence of the civil lift only, for the fupport of one man, is eight times greater than the whole expence of the federal government in America. To affign a reafon for this, appears almoft impoffible. The generality of people in America, efpecially the poor, are more able to pay taxes, than the generality of people either in France or England.

But the cafe is, that the reprefentative fyftem diffufes fuch a body of knowledge throughout a nation, on the fubject of government, as to ex-plode ignorance and preclude impofition. The craft of courts cannot be acted on that ground. There is no place for myftery; no where for it to begin. Thofe who are not in the reprefentation, know as much of the nature of bufinefs as thofe

who

who are. An affectation of myfterious importance would there be fcouted. Nations can have
no fecrets; and the fecrets of courts, like thofe
of individuals, are always their defects.

In the reprefentative fyftem, the reafon for
every thing muft publicly appear. Every man
is a proprietor in government, and confiders
it a neceffary part of his bufinefs to underftand.
It concerns his intereft, becaufe it affects his
property. He examines the coft, and com-
pares it with the advantages; and above all, he
does not adopt the flavifh cuftom of following
what in other governments are called LEADERS.

It can only be by blinding the underftanding of
man, and making him believe that government
is fome wonderful myfterious thing, that exceffive
revenues are obtained. Monarchy is well calculated to enfure this end. It is the popery of
government; a thing kept up to amufe the ignorant, and quiet them into taxes.

The government of a free country, properly
fpeaking, is not in the perfons, but in the laws.
The enacting of thofe requires no great expence;
and when they are adminiftered, the whole of
civil government is performed—the reft is all
court contrivance.

CHAP.

CHAP. IV.

OF CONSTITUTIONS.

THAT men mean diftinct and feparate things when they fpeak of conftitutions and of governments, is evident; or, why are thofe terms diftinctly and feparately ufed? A conftitution is not the act of a government, but of a people conftituting a government; and government without a conftitution, is power without a right.

All power exercifed over a nation, muft have fome beginning. It muft be either delegated, or affumed. There are no other fources. All delegated power is truft, and all affumed power is ufurpation. Time does not alter the nature and quality of either.

In viewing this fubject, the cafe and circumftances of America prefent themfelves as in the beginning of a world; and our enquiry into the origin of government is fhortened, by referring to the facts that have arifen in our own day. We have no occafion to roam for information into the obfcure field of antiquity, nor hazard ourfelves upon conjecture. We are brought at once to the point of feeing government begin, as if we had lived in the beginning of time. The real volume, not of
hiftory,

hiftory, but of facts, is directly before us, unmutilated by contrivance, or the errors of tradition.

I will here concifely ftate the commencement of the American conftitutions; by which the difference between conftitutions and governments will fufficiently appear.

It may not be improper to remind the reader, that the United States of America confift of thirteen feparate ftates, each of which eftablifhed a government for itfelf, after the declaration of independence, done the fourth of July 1776. Each ftate acted independently of the reft, in forming its government; but the fame general principle pervades the whole. When the feveral ftate governments were formed, they proceeded to form the federal government, that acts over the whole in all matters which concern the intereft of the whole, or which relate to the intercourfe of the feveral ftates with each other, or with foreign nations. I will begin with giving an inftance from one of the ftate governments, (that of Pennfylvania), and then proceed to the federal government.

The ftate of Pennfylvania, though nearly of the fame extent of territory as England, was then divided into only twelve counties. Each of thofe counties had elected a committee at the commencement of the difpute with the Englifh government; and as the city of Philadelphia, which alfo had its committee, was the moft central for intelligence, it became the center of communication to the feveral county committees.
When

When it became neceffary to proceed to the
formation of a government, the committee of
Philadelphia propofed a conference of all the
county committees, to be held in that city, and
which met the latter end of July 1776.

Though thefe committees had been elected by
the people, they were not elected exprefsly for the
purpofe, nor invefted with the authority, of forming a conftitution; and as they could not, con-
fiftently with the American idea of rights, affume
fuch a power, they could only confer upon the
matter, and put it into a train of operation. The
conferrees, therefore, did no more than ftate the
cafe, and recommend to the feveral counties to
elect fix reprefentatives for each county, to meet
in convention at Philadelphia, with powers to
form a conftitution, and propofe it for public
confideration.

This convention, of which Benjamin Franklin
was prefident, having met and deliberated, and
agreed upon a conftitution, they next ordered it
to be publifhed, not as a thing eftablifhed, but
for the confideration of the whole people, their
approbation or rejection, and then adjourned to
a ftated time. When the time of adjournment
was expired, the convention re-affembled; and
as the general opinion of the people in approbation of it was then known, the conftitution was
figned, fealed, and proclaimed on the *authority
of the people* and the original inftrument
depofited as a public record. The convention
then appointed a day for the general election of
the reprefentatives who were to compofe the
government,

government, and the time it fhould commence;
and having done this, they diffolved, and returned
to their feveral homes and occupations.

In this conftitution were laid down, firft, a
declaration of rights. Then followed the form
which the government fhould have, and the
powers it fhould poffefs—the authority of the
courts of judicature, and of juries—the manner
in which elections fhould be conducted, and the
proportion of reprefentatives to the number of
electors—the time which each fucceeding affembly fhould continue, which was one year—the
mode of levying, and of accounting for the expenditure, of public money—of appointing public
officers, &c. &c. &c.

No article of this conftitution could be altered
or infringed at the difcretion of the government
that was to enfue.   It was to that government a
law.   But as it would have been unwife, to preclude the benefit of experience, and in order
alfo to prevent the accumulation of errors, if any
fhould be found, and to preferve an unifon of
government with the circumftances of the ftate at
all times, the conftitution provided, that, at the
expiration of every feven years, a convention
fhould be elected, for the exprefs purpofe of
revifing the conftitution, and making alterations,
additions, or abolitions therein, if any fuch fhould
be found neceffary.

Here we fee a regular procefs—a government iffuing out of a conftitution, formed by the
people in their original character; and that conftitution ferving, not only as an authority, but as
a law

a law of controul to the government. It was the political bible of the ftate. Scarcely a family was without it. Every member of the government had a copy ; and nothing was more common, when any debate arofe on the principle of a bill, or on the extent of any fpecies of authority, than for the members to take the printed conftitution out of their pocket, and read the chapter with which fuch matter in debate was connected.

Having thus given an inftance from one of the ftates, I will fhew the proceedings by which the federal conftitution of the United States arofe and was formed.

Congrefs, at its two firft meetings, in September 1774, and May 1775, was nothing more than a deputation from the legiflatures of the feveral provinces, afterwards ftates ; and had no other authority than what arofe from common confent, and the neceffity of its acting as a public body. In every thing which related to the internal affairs of America, congrefs went no further than to iffue recommendations to the feveral provincial affemblies, who at difcretion adopted them or not. Nothing on the part of congrefs was compulfive ; yet, in this fituation, it was more faithfully and affectionately obeyed, than was any government in Europe. This inftance, like that of the national affembly in France, fufficiently fhews, that the ftrength of government does not confift in any thing *within* itfelf, but in the attachment of a nation, and the intereft which the people feel in fupporting it. When this

3   is

is loft, government is but a child in power; and though, like the old government of France, it may harrafs individuals for a while, it but facilitates its own fall.

After the declaration of independence, it became confiftent with the principle on which reprefentative government is founded, that the authority of congrefs fhould be defined and eftablifhed. Whether that authority fhould be more or lefs than congrefs then difcretionarily exercifed, was not the queftion. It was merely the rectitude of the meafure.

For this purpofe, the act, called the act of confederation, (which was a fort of imperfect federal conftitution), was propofed, and, after long deliberation, was concluded in the year 1781. It was not the act of congrefs, becaufe it is repugnant to the principles of reprefentative government that a body fhould give power to itfelf. Congrefs firft informed the feveral ftates, of the powers which it conceived were neceffary to be invefted in the union, to enable it to perform the duties and fervices required from it; and the ftates feverally agreed with each other, and concenterated in congrefs thofe powers.

It may not be improper to obferve, that in both thofe inftances, (the one of Pennfylvania, and the other of the United States), there is no fuch thing as the idea of a compact between the people on one fide, and the government on the other. The compact was that of the people with each other, to produce and conftitute a
government.

government. To suppose that any government can be a party in a compact with the whole people, is to suppose it to have existence before it can have a right to exist. The only instance in which a compact can take place between the people and those who exercise the government, is, that the people shall pay them, while they chuse to employ them.

Government is not a trade which any man or body of men has a right to set up and exercise for his own emolument, but is altogether a trust, in right of those by whom that trust is delegated, and by whom it is always resumeable. It has of itself no rights; they are altogether duties.

Having thus given two instances of the original formation of a constitution, I will shew the manner in which both have been changed since their first establishment.

The powers vested in the governments of the several states, by the state constitutions, were found, upon experience, to be too great; and those vested in the federal government, by the act of confederation, too little. The defect was not in the principle, but in the distribution of power.

Numerous publications, in pamphlets and in the newspapers, appeared, on the propriety and necessity of new modelling the federal government. After some time of public discussion, carried on through the channel of the press, and in conversations, the state of Virginia, experiencing some inconvenience with respect to commerce, pro posed holding a continental conference; in conse-

2   quence

quence of which, a deputation from five or six of the state affemblies met at Anapolis in Maryland, in 1786. This meeting, not conceiving itfelf fufficiently authorifed to go into the bufinefs of a reform, did no more than ftate their general opinions of the propriety of the meafure, and recommend that a convention of all the ftates fhould be held the year following.

This convention met at Philadelphia in May 1787, of which General Wafhington was elected prefident. He was not at that time connected with any of the ftate governments, or with congrefs. He delivered up his commiffion when the war ended, and fince then had lived a private citizen.

The convention went deeply into all the fubjects; and having, after a variety of debate and inveftigation, agreed among themfelves upon the feveral parts of a federal conftitution, the next queftion was, the manner of giving it authority and practice.

For this purpofe, they did not, like a cabal of courtiers, fend for a Dutch Stadtholder, or a German Elector; but they referred the whole matter to the fenfe and intereft of the country.

They firft directed, that the propofed conftitution fhould be publifhed. Secondly, that each ftate fhould elect a convention, exprefsly for the purpofe of taking it into confideration, and of ratifying or rejecting it; and that as foon as the approbation and ratification of any nine ftates fhould be given, that thofe ftates fhould proceed to the election of their proportion of members to
the

the new federal government ; and that the operation of it fhould then begin, and the former
federal government ceafe.

The feveral ftates proceeded accordingly to
elect their conventions. Some of thofe conventions ratified the conftitution by very large ma-
jorities, and two or three unanimoufly. In others
there were much debate and divifion of opinion.
In the Maffachufetts convention, which met at
Bofton, the majority was not above nineteen or
twenty, in about three hundred members; but
fuch is the nature of reprefentative government,
that it quietly decides all matters by majority.
After the debate in the Maffachufetts convention
was clofed, and the vote taken, the objecting members rofe, and declared, *"That though they had argued*
" and voted againft it, becaufe certain parts appeared
" to them in a different light to what they appeared
" to other members; yet, as the vote had decided in
" favour of the conftitution as propofed, they fhould
" give it the fame practical fupport as if they had
" voted for it."

As foon as nine ftates had concurred, (and the
reft followed in the order their conventions were
elected), the old fabric of the federal government
was taken down, and the new one erected, of
which General Wafhington is prefident.—In this
place I cannot help remarking, that the character
and fervices of this gentleman are fufficient to put
all thofe men called kings to fhame. While they
are receiving from the fweat and labours of mankind, a prodigality of pay, to which neither their

abilities

abilities nor their fervices can entitle them, he is rendering every fervice in his power, and refufing every pecuniary reward. He accepted no pay as commander in chief; he accepts none as prefident of the United States.

After the new federal conftitution was eftablifhed, the ftate of Pennfylvania, conceiving that fome parts of its own conftitution required to be altered, elected a convention for that purpofe. The propofed alterations were publifhed, and the people concurring therein, they were eftablifhed.

In forming thofe conftitutions, or in altering them, little or no inconvenience took place. The ordinary courfe of things was not interrupted, and the advantages have been much. It is always the intereft of a far greater number of people in a nation to have things right, than to let them remain wrong; and when public matters are open to debate, and the public judgment free, it will not decide wrong, unlefs it decides too haftily.

In the two inftances of changing the conftitutions, the governments then in being were not actors either way. Government has no right to make itfelf a party in any debate refpecting the principles or modes of forming, or of changing, conftitutions. It is not for the benefit of thofe who exercife the powers of government, that conftitutions, and the governments iffuing from them, are eftablifhed. In all thofe matters, the right of judging and acting are in thofe who pay, and not in thofe who receive.

A conftitution is the property of a nation, and
E not

not of thofe who exercife the government. All the
conftitutions of America are declared to be eftablifhed on the authority of the people.   In France,
the word nation is ufed inftead of the people; but
in both cafes, a conftitution is a thing antecedent
to the government, and always diftinct therefrom.

In England, it is not difficult to perceive that
every thing has a conftitution, except the nation.
Every fociety and affociation that is eftablifhed,
firft agreed upon a number of original articles,
digefted into form, which are its conftitution.   It
then appointed its officers, whofe powers and
authorities are defcribed in that conftitution, and
the government of that fociety then commenced.
Thofe officers, by whatever name they are called,
have no authority to add to, alter, or abridge the
original articles.   It is only to the conftituting
power that this right belongs.

From the want of underftanding the difference
between a conftitution and a government, Dr.
Johnfon, and all writers of his defcription, have
always bewildered themfelves.   They could not
but perceive, that there muft neceffarily be a
controuling power exifting fomewhere, and they
placed this power in the difcretion of the perfons
exercifing the government, inftead of placing it in
a conftitution formed by the nation.   When it is
in a conftitution, it has the nation for its fupport,
and the natural and the political controuling
powers are together.   The laws which are enacted
by governments, controul men only as individuals,
but

but the nation, through its conſtitution, controuls the whole government, and has a natural ability ſo to do.   The final controuling power, therefore, and the original conſtituting power, are one and the ſame power.

Dr. Johnſon could not have advanced ſuch a poſition in any country where there was a conſtitution; and he is himſelf an evidence, that no ſuch thing as a conſtitution exiſts in England.—But it may be put as a queſtion, not improper to be inveſtigated, That if a conſtitution does not exiſt, how came the idea of its exiſtence ſo generally eſtabliſhed?

In order to decide this queſtion, it is neceſſary to conſider a conſtitution in both its caſes :—Firſt, as creating a government and giving it powers. Secondly, as regulating and reſtraining the powers ſo given.

If we begin with William of Normandy, we find that the government of England was originally a tyranny, founded on an invaſion and conqueſt of the country.   This being admitted, it will then appear, that the exertion of the nation, at different periods, to abate that tyranny, and render it leſs intolerable, has been credited for a conſtitution.

Magna Charta, as it was called, (it is now like an almanack of the ſame date,) was no more than compelling the government to renounce a part of its aſſumptions.   It did not create and give powers to government in the manner a conſtitution does; but was, as far as it went, of the

nature

nature of a re-conqueft, and not of a conftitution; for could the nation have totally expelled the ufurpation, as France has done its defpotifm, it would then have had a conftitution to form.

The hiftory of the Edwards and the Henries, and up to the commencement of the Stuarts, exhibits as many inftances of tyranny as could be acted within the limits to which the nation had reftricted it. The Stuarts endeavoured to pafs thofe limits, and their fate is well known. In all thofe inftances we fee nothing of a conftitution, but only of reftrictions on affumed power.

After this, another William, defcended from the fame ftock, and claiming from the fame origin, gained poffeffion; and of the two evils, *James* and *William*, the nation preferred what it thought the leaft; fince, from circumftances, it muft take one. The act, called the Bill of Rights, comes here into view. What is it, but a bargain, which the parts of the government made with each other to divide powers, profits, and privileges? You fhall have fo much, and I will have the reft; and with refpect to the nation, it faid, for *your fhare,* YOU *fhall have the right of petitioning.* This being the cafe, the bill of rights is more properly a bill of wrongs, and of infult. As to what is called the convention parliament, it was a thing that made itfelf, and then made the authority by which it acted. A few perfons got together, and called themfelves by that name. Several of them had never been elected, and none of them for the purpofe.

From the time of William, a fpecies of govern- ment

ment arofe, iffuing out of this coalition bill of
rights; and more fo, fince the corruption introduced at the Hanover fucceffion, by the agency
of Walpole; that can be defcribed by no other
name than a defpotic legiflation.   Though the
parts may embarrafs each other, the whole has no
bounds; and the only right it acknowledges out
of itfelf, is the right of petitioning.   Where then
is the conftitution either that gives or that reftrains
power?

It is not becaufe a part of the government is
elective, that makes it lefs a defpotifm, if the
perfons fo elected, poffefs afterwards, as a parliament, unlimited powers.   Election, in this cafe,
becomes feparated from reprefentation, and the
candidates are candidates for defpotifm.

I cannot believe that any nation, reafoning on
its own rights, would have thought of calling
thofe things *a conftitution*, if the cry of conftitution had not been fet up by the government.   It
has got into circulation like the words *bore* and
quoz, by being chalked up in the fpeeches of
parliament, as thofe words were on window fhut-
ters and door pofts; but whatever the conftitution may be in other refpects, it has undoubtedly
been *the moft productive machine of taxation that
was ever invented.*   The taxes in France, under
the new conftitution, are not quite thirteen
fhillings per head*, and the taxes in England,
under

* The whole amount of the affeffed taxes of France, for the
prefent year, is three hundred millions of livres, which is twelve

E 3   millions

under what is called its prefent conftitution, are forty-eight fhillings and fixpence per head, men, women, and children, amounting to nearly feventeen millions fterling, befides the expence of collection, which is upwards of a million more.

In a country like England, where the whole of the civil government is executed by the people of every town and county, by means of parifh officers, magiftrates, quarterly feffions, juries, and affize; without any trouble to what is called the government, or any other expence to the revenue than the falary of the judges, it is aftonifhing how fuch a mafs of taxes can be employed. Not even the internal defence of the country is paid out of the revenue. On all occafions, whether real or con trived, recourfe is continually had to new loans and new taxes. No wonder, then, that a machine of government fo advantageous to the advocates of a court, fhould be fo triumphantly extolled! No wonder, that St. James's or St. Stephen's fhould echo with the continual cry of conftitution! No wonder, that the French revolution fhould be reprobated, and the *res-publica* treated with reproach! The *red*

millions and a half fterling; and the incidental taxes are eftimated at three millions, making in the whole fifteen millions and a half; which, among twenty-four millions of people, is not quite thirteen fhillings per head. France has leffened her taxes fince the revolution, nearly nine millions fterling annually. Before the revolution, the city of Paris paid a duty of upwards of thirty per cent. on all articles brought into the city. This tax was collected at the city gates. It was taken off on the firft of laft May, and the gates taken down.

book of England, like the red book of France, will explain the reafon *.

I will now, by way of relaxation, turn a thought or two to Mr. Burke.   I afk his pardon for neg-lecting him fo long.

"America," fays he, (in his fpeech on the Canada conftitution bill) " never dreamed of " fuch abfurd doctrine as the *Rights of Man*."

Mr. Burke is fuch a bold prefumer, and ad-vances his affertions and his premifes with fuch a deficiency of judgment, that, without troubling ourfelves about principles of philofophy or politics, the mere logical conclufions they pro-duce, are ridiculous.   For inftance,

If governments, as Mr. Burke afferts, are not founded on the Rights of MAN, and are founded on *any rights* at all, they confequently. muft be founded on the rights of *fomething* that is *not man*. What then is that fomething?

Generally fpeaking, we know of no other creatures that inhabit the earth than man and beaft; and in all cafes, where only two things offer themfelves, and one muft be admitted, a negation proved on any one, amounts to an affir-mative on the other ; and therefore, Mr. Burke, by proving againft the Rights of *Man*, proves in

---

* What was called the *livre rouge*, or the red book, in France, was not exactly fimilar to the court calendar in England ; but it fufficiently fhewed how a great part of the taxes was lavifhed.

behalf

behalf of the *beaft*; and confequently, proves that
government is a beaft : and as difficult things
fometimes explain each other, we now fee the
origin of keeping wild beafts in the Tower; for
they certainly can be of no other ufe than to fhew
the origin of the government   They are in the
place of a conftitution.   O John Bull, what
honours thou haft loft by not being a wild beaft.
Thou mighteft, on Mr. Burke's fyftem, have
been in the Tower for life.

If Mr. Burke's arguments have not weight
enough to keep one ferious, the fault is lefs mine
than his; and as I am willing to make an apology
to the reader for the liberty I have taken, I hope
Mr. Burke will alfo make his for giving the caufe.

Having thus paid Mr. Burke the compliment
of remembering him, I return to the fubject.

From the want of a conftitution in England to
reftrain and regulate the wild impulfe of power,
many of the laws are irrational and tyrannical,
and the adminiftration of them vague and pro-
blematical.

The attention of the government of England,
(for I rather chufe to call it by this name, than
the Englifh government)   appears, fince its
political connection with Germany, to have been
fo compleatly engroffed and abforbed by foreign
affairs, and the means of raifing taxes, that it
feems to exift for no other purpofes.   Domeftic
concerns are neglected; and, with refpect to regular
law, there is fcarcely fuch a thing.

Almoft

Almoft every cafe now muft be determined by
fome precedent, be that precedent good or bad, or
whether it properly applies or not; and the practice is become fo general, as to fuggeft a fufpicion,
that it proceeds from a deeper policy than at firft
fight appears.

Since the revolution of America, and more fo
fince that of France, this preaching up the doctrine
of precedents, drawn from times and circumftances
antecedent to thofe events, has been the ftudied
practice of the Englifh government. The generality of thofe precedents are founded on principles and opinions, the reverfe of what they
ought; and the greater diftance of time they are
drawn from, the more they are to be fufpected:
But by affociating thofe precedents with a fuper-
ftitious reverence for ancient things, as monks
fhew relics and call them holy, the generality of
mankind are deceived into the defign. Governments now act as if they were afraid to awaken a
fingle reflection in man. They are foftly leading
him to the fepulchre of precedents, to deaden his
faculties and call his attention from the fcene of
revolutions. They feel that he is arriving at
knowledge fafter than they wifh, and their
policy of precedents is the barometer of their
fears. This political popery, like the ecclefiaftical
popery of old, has had its day, and is haftening to
its exit. The ragged relic and the antiquated
precedent, the monk and the monarch, will moul-
der together.

Government by precedent, without any regard
                                            to

to the principle of the precedent, is one of the
vileſt ſyſtems that can be ſet up. In numerous
inſtances, the precedent ought to operate as a
warning, and not as an example, and requires to
be ſhunned inſtead of imitated; but inſtead of
this, precedents are taken in the lump, and put
at once for conſtitution and for law.

Either the doctrine of precedents is policy to
keep man in a ſtate of ignorance, or it is a practical confeſſion that wiſdom degenerates in governments as governments increaſe in age, and can
only hobble along by the ſtilts and crutches of
precedents.   How. is it that the ſame perſons
who would proudly be thought wiſer than their
predeceſſors, appear at the ſame time only as the
ghoſts of departed wiſdom? How ſtrangely is antiquity treated!   To anſwer ſome purpoſes it is
ſpoken of as the times of darkneſs and ignorance,
and to anſwer others, it is put for the light of the
world.

If the doctrine of precedents, is to be followed,
the expences of government need not continue
the ſame.   Why pay men extravagantly, who
have but little to do? If every thing that can
happen is already in precedent, legiſlation is at an
end, and precedent, like a dictionary, determines
every caſe.   Either, therefore, government .has
arrived at its dotage, and requires to be reno-
vated, or all the occaſions for exerciſing its wiſdom
have occured.

We now ſee all over Europe, and particularly
in England, the curious phænomenon of a nation
looking

looking one way, and a government the other—
the one forward and the other backward. If
governments are to go on by precedent, while
nations go on by improvement, they muſt at laſt
come to a final ſeparation; and the ſooner, and
the more civilly, they determine this point, the
better *.

Having thus ſpoken of conſtitutions generally,
as things diſtinct from actual governments, let us
proceed to conſider the parts of which a conſtitution is compoſed.

Opinions differ more on this ſubject, than with
reſpect to the whole. That a nation ought to
have a conſtitution, as a rule for the conduct of
its government, is a ſimple queſtion in which all
men, not directly courtiers, will agree. It is only
on the component parts that queſtions and opinions multiply.

* In England, the improvements in agriculture, uſeful arts,
manufactures, and commerce, have been made in oppoſition to
the genius of its government, which is that of following precedents. It is from the enterprize and induſtry of the individuals,
and their numerous aſſociations, in which, tritely ſpeaking,
government is neither pillow nor bolſter, that theſe improve
ments have proceeded. No man thought about the government, or who was *in*, or who was *out*, when he was planning
or executing thoſe things; and all he had to hope, with reſpect to
government, was, *that it would let him alone*. Three or four very
ſilly miniſterial news-papers are continually offending againſt the
ſpirit of national improvement, by aſcribing it to a miniſter.
They may with as much truth aſcribe this book to a miniſter.

But

But this difficulty, like every other, will diminish when put into a train of being rightly underftood.

The firft thing is, that a nation has a right to eftablifh a conftitution.

Whether it exercifes this right in the moft judicious manner at firft, is quite another cafe. It exercifes it agreeably to the judgment it poffeffes; and by continuing to do fo, all errors will at laft be exploded.

When this right is eftablifhed in a nation, there is no fear that it will be employed to its own injury. A nation can have no intereft in being wrong.

Though all the conftitutions of America are on one general principle, yet no two of them are exactly alike in their component parts, or in the diftribution of the powers which they give to the actual governments. Some are more, and others lefs complex.

In forming a conftitution, it is firft neceffary to confider what are the ends for which government is neceffary? Secondly, what are the beft means, and the leaft expenfive, for accomplifhing thofe ends?

Government is nothing more than a national affociation; and the object of this affociation is the good of all, as well individually as collectively. Every man wifhes to purfue his occupation, and to enjoy the fruits of his labours, and the produce of his property in peace and fafety, and with the leaft poffible expence. When thefe

things

things are accomplifhed, all the objects for which government ought to be eftablifhed are anfwered.

It has been cuftomary to confider government under three diftinct general heads. The legiflative, the executive, and the judicial.

But if we permit our judgment to act unincumbered by the habit of multiplied terms, we can perceive no more than two divifions of power, of which civil government is compofed, namely, that of legiflating or enacting laws, and that of executing or adminiftering them. Every thing, therefore, appertaining to civil government, claffes itfelf under one or other of thefe two divifions.

So far as regards the execution of the laws, that which is called the judicial power, is ftrictly and properly the executive power of every country. It is that power to which every individual has appeal, and which caufes the laws to be executed; neither have we any other clear idea with refpect to the official execution of the laws. In England, and alfo in America and France, this power begins with the magiftrate, and proceeds up through all the courts of judicature.

I leave to courtiers to explain what is meant by calling monarchy the executive power. It is merely a name in which acts of government are done; and any other, or none at all, would anfwer the fame purpofe. Laws have neither more nor lefs authority on this account. It muft be from the juftnefs of their principles, and the intereft which a nation feels therein, that they derive fupport; if

I   they

they require any other than this, it is a sign that something in the system of government is imperfect. Laws difficult to be executed cannot be generally good.

With respect to the organization of the *legislative power*, different modes have been adopted in different countries. In America it is generally composed of two houses. In France it consists but of one, but in both countries it is wholly by representation.

The case is, that mankind (from the long tyranny of assumed power) have had so few opportunities of making the necessary trials on modes and principles of government, in order to discover the best, *that government is but now beginning to be known*, and experience is yet wanting to determine many particulars.

The objections against two houses are, first, that there is an inconsistency in any part of a whole legislature, coming to a final determination by vote on any matter, whilst *that matter*, with respect to *that whole*, is yet only in a train of deliberation, and consequently open to new illustrations.

Secondly, That by taking the vote on each, as a separate body, it always admits of the possibility, and is often the case in practice, that the minority governs the majority, and that, in some instances, to a degree of great inconsistency.

Thirdly, That two houses arbitrarily checking or controuling each other is inconsistent; because it

    cannot

cannot be proved, on the principles of juſt repreſentation, that either ſhould be wiſer or better than the
other. They may check in the wrong as well as
in the right,—and therefore, to give the power
where we cannot give the wiſdom to uſe it, nor be
aſſured of its being rightly uſed, renders the
hazard at leaſt equal to the precaution *

* With reſpect to the two houſes, of which the Engliſh Parliament is compoſed, they appear to be effectually influenced
into one, and, as a legiſlature, to have no temper of its own.
The miniſter, whoever he at any time may be, touches it as with
an opium wand, and it ſleeps obedience.

But if we look at the diſtinct abilities of the two houſes, the
difference will appear ſo great, as to ſhew the inconſiſtency of
placing power where there can be no certainty of the judgment.
to uſe it. Wretched as the ſtate of repreſentation is in England, it is manhood compared with what is called the houſe of
Lords ; and ſo little is this nick-named houſe regarded, that the
people ſcarcely inquire at any time what it is doing. It appears alſo to be moſt under influence, and the furtheſt removed
from the general intereſt of the nation. In the debate on en-
gaging in the Ruſſian and Turkiſh war, the majority in the
houſe of peers in favour of it was upwards of ninety, when in
the other houſe, which is more than double its numbers, the
majority was ſixty-three.

The proceedings on Mr. Fox's bill, reſpecting the rights of
juries, merits alſo to be noticed. The perſons called the peers
were not the objects of that bill. They are already in poſſeſſion
of more privileges than that bill gave to others. They are
their own jury, and if any of that houſe were proſecuted for a
libel, he would not ſuffer, even upon conviction, for the firſt
offence. Such inequality in laws ought not to exiſt in any
country. The French conſtitution ſays, That *the law is the
ſame to every individual, whether to protect or to puniſh. All are
equal in its ſight.*

The

The objection against a single house is, that it is always in a condition of committing itself too soon.—But it should at the same time be remembered, that when there is a conftitution which defines the power, and establishes the principles within which a legiflature shall act, there is already a more effectual check provided, and more powerfully operating, than any other check can be. For example,

Were a bill to be brought into any of the American legiflatures, fimilar to that which was paffed into an act by the Englifh parliament, at the commencement of George the Firft, to extend the duration of the affemblies to a longer period than they now fit, the check is in the conftitution, which in effect fays, *Thus far fhalt thou go and no further.*

But in order to remove the objection against a fingle houfe, (that of acting with too quick an impulfe,) and at the fame time to avoid the inconfiftencies, in fome cafes abfurdities, arifing from two houfes, the following method has been propofed as an improvement upon both.

Firft, To have but one reprefentation.

Secondly, To divide that reprefentation, by lot, into two or three parts.

Thirdly, That every propofed bill, fhall be firft debated in thofe parts by fucceffion, that they may become the hearers of each other, but without taking any vote.   After which the whole reprefentation

fentation to affemble for a general debate and de-termination by vote.

To this propofed improvement has been added another, for the purpofe of keeping the reprefen-tation in a ftate of conftant renovation; which is, that one-third of the reprefentation of each county, fhall go out at the expiration of one year, and the number be replaced by new elections.—Another third at the expiration of the fecond year replaced in like manner, and every third year to be a ge-neral election *

But in whatever manner the feparate parts of a conftitution may be arranged, there is *one* general principle that diftinguifhes freedom from flavery, which is, that all *hereditary government over a people is to them a fpecies of flavery, and reprefen-tative government is freedom.*

Confidering government in the only light in which it fhould be confidered, that of a NA-TIONAL ASSOCIATION; it ought to be fo con-ftructed as not to be difordered by any accident happening among the parts; and, therefore, no extraordinary power, capable of producing fuch an effect, fhould be lodged in the hands of any indi-vidual. The death, ficknefs, abfence, or defec-

---

* As to the ftate of reprefentation in England, it is too abfurd to be reafoned upon. Almoft all the reprefented parts are decreafing in population, and the unreprefented parts are increafing. A general convention of the nation is neceffary to take the whole ftate of its government into confideration.

tion

tion, of any one individual in a government, ought to be a matter of no more confequence, with refpect to the nation, than if the fame circumftance had taken place in a member of the Englifh Parliament, or the French National Affembly.

Scarcely any thing prefents a more degrading character of national greatnefs, than its being thrown into confufion by any thing happening to, or acted by, an individual; and the ridiculoufnefs of the fcene is often increafed by the natural infignificance of the perfon by whom it is occafioned. Were a government fo conftructed, that it could not go on unlefs a goofe or a gander were prefent in the fenate, the difficulties would be juft as great and as real on the flight or ficknefs of the goofe, or the gander, as if it were called a King. We laugh at individuals for the filly difficulties they make to themfelves, without perceiving, that the greateft of all ridiculous things are acted in governments *.

All

---

* It is related, that in the canton of Berne, in Swifferland, it had been cuftomary, from time immemorial, to keep a bear at the public expence, and the people had been taught to believe, that if they had not a bear they fhould all be undone. It happened fome years ago, that the bear, then in being, was taken fick and died too fuddenly to have his place immediately fupplied with another. During this interregnum the people difcovered, that the corn grew, and the vintage flourifhed, and the fun and moon continued to rife and fet, and every thing went on the fame as before, and, taking courage from thefe circumftances,

All the conftitutions of America are on a plan that excludes the childifh embarraffments which occur in monarchical countries. No fufpenfion of government can there take place for a moment, from any circumftance whatever. The fyflem of reprefentation provides for every thing, and is the only fyftem in which nations and governments can always appear in their proper character.

As extraordinary power, ought not to be lodged in the hands of any individual, fo ought there to be no appropriations of public money to any perfon, beyond what his fervices in a ftate may be worth. It fignifies not whether a man be called a prefident, a king, an emperor, a fenator, or by any other name, which propriety or folly may devife, or arrogance affume, it is only a certain fervice he can perform in the ftate; and the fervice of any fuch individual in the rotine of office, whether fuch office be called monarchical, prefidential, fenatorial, or by any other name or title, can never exceed the value of ten thoufand

---

cumftances, they refolved not to keep any more bears; for faid they, " a bear is a very voracious, expenfive animal, and " we were obliged to pull out his claws, left he fhould hurt the " citizens."

The ftory of the bear of Berne was related in fome of the French news-papers, at the time of the flight of Louis XVI. and the application of it to monarchy could not be miftaken in France; but it feems, that the ariftocracy of Berne applied it to themfelves, and have fince prohibited the reading of French news-papers.

pounds

pounds a year. All the great fervices that are
done in the world are performed by volunteer
characters, who accept nothing for them; but
the rotine of office is always regulated to fuch a
general ftandard of abilities as to be within
the compafs of numbers in every country to perform, and therefore cannot merit very extraordinary recompence. *Government,* fays Swift, *is a
plain thing, and fitted to the capacity of many
heads.*

It is inhuman to talk of a million fterling a
year, paid out of the public taxes of any country,
for the fupport of any individual, whilft thoufands
who are forced to contribute thereto, are pining
with want, and ftruggling with mifery. Government does not confift in a contraft between prifons
and palaces, between poverty and pomp; it is
not inftituted to rob the needy of his mite, and
increafe the wretchednefs of the wretched.—But
of this part of the fubject I fhall fpeak hereafter,
and confine myfelf at prefent to political obfervations.

When extraordinary power and extraordinary
pay are allotted to any individual in a government, he becomes the center, round which every
kind of corruption generates and forms. Give
to any man a million a year, and add thereto the
power of creating and difpofing of places, at the
expence of a country, and the liberties of that
country are no longer fecure. What is called the
fplendor of a throne is no other than the corrup-

2   tion

tion of the ſtate.   It is made up of a band of pa-
raſites, living in luxurious indolence, out of the
public taxes.

When once ſuch a vicious ſyſtem is eſtabliſhed
it becomes the guard and protection of all in erior
abuſes.   The man who is in the receipt of a million a year is the laſt perſon to promote a ſpirit of
reform, left, in the event, it ſhould reach to himſelf.   It is always his intereſt to defend inferior
abuſes, as ſo many out-works to protect the cita-
del; and in this ſpecies of political fortification,
all the parts have ſuch a common dependence that
it is never to be expected they will attack each
other *.

Monarchy

* It is ſcarcely poſſible to touch on any ſubject, that will
not ſuggeſt an alluſion to ſome corruption in governments.   The
ſimile of "*fortifications*," unfortunately involves with it a cir-
cumſtance, which is directly in point with the matter above
alluded to.

Among the numerous iuſtances of abuſe which have been acted
or protected by governments, ancient or modern, there is not a
greater than that of quartering a man and his heirs upon the
public, to be maintained at its expence.

Humanity dictates a proviſion for the poor ; but by what right,
moral or political, does any government aſſume to ſay, that the
perſon called the Duke of Richmond, ſhall be maintained by the
public ? Yet, if common report is true, not a beggar in London can
purchaſe his wretched pittance of coal, without paying towards
the civil liſt of the Duke of Richmond. Were the whole produce
of this impoſition but a ſhilling a year, the iniquitous principle
would be ſtill the ſame ; but when it amounts, as it is ſaid to do,
to not leſs than twenty thouſand pounds *per ann.* the enor-
mity is too ſerious to be permitted to remain—This is one of the
effects of monarchy and ariſtocracy.

F 3   In

Monarchy would not have continued so many ages in the world, had it not been for the abuses it protects. It is the master fraud, which shelters all others. By admitting a participation of the spoil, it makes itself friends; and when it ceases to do this, it will cease to be the idol of courtiers.

As the principle on which constitutions are now formed rejects all hereditary pretentions to government, it also rejects all that catalogue of assumptions known by the name of prerogatives.

If there is any government where prerogatives might with apparent safety be entrusted to any individual, it is in the fœderal government of America. The President of the United States of America is elected only for four years.. He is not only responsible in the general sense of the word, but a particular mode is laid down in the constitution for trying him. He cannot be elected under thirty-five years of age; and he must be a native of the country.

In a comparison of these cases with the government of England, the difference when applied to the latter amounts to an absurdity. In England the person who exercises prerogative is often a

---

In stating this case, I am led by no personal dislike. Though I think it mean in any man to live upon the public, the vice originates in the government; and so general is it become, that whether the parties are in the ministry or in the opposition, it makes no difference : they are sure of the guarantee of each other.

foreigner;

foreigner; always half a foreigner, and always married to a foreigner. He is never in full natural or political connection with the country, is not refponfible for any thing, and becomes of age at eighteen years; yet fuch a perfon is permitted to form foreign alliances, without even the knowledge of the nation, and to make war and peace without its confent.

But this is not all. Though fuch a perfon cannot difpofe of the government, in the manner of a teftator, he dictates the marriage connections, which, in effect, accomplifhes a great part of the fame end. He cannot directly bequeath half the government to Pruffia, but he can form a marriage partnerfhip that will produce almoft the fame thing. Under fuch circumftances, it is happy for England that fhe is not fituated on the continent, or fhe might, like Holland, fall under the dictatorfhip of Pruffia. Holland, by marriage, is as effectually governed by Pruffia, as if the old tyranny of bequeathing the government had been the means.

The prefidency in America, (or, as it is fometimes called, the executive,) is the only office from which a foreigner is excluded, and in England it is the only one to which he is admitted. A foreigner cannot be a member of parliament, but he may be what is called a king. If there is any reafon for excluding foreigners, it ought to be from thofe offices where mifchief can moft be acted, and where, by uniting every

F 4   bias

bias of intereſt and attachment, the truſt is beſt
ſecured.

But as nations proceed in the great buſineſs
of forming conſtitutions, they will examine with
more preciſion into the nature and buſineſs of
that department which is called the executive.
What the legiſlative and judicial departments are,
every one can ſee; but with reſpect to what, in
Europe, is called the executive, as diſtinct from
thoſe two, it is either a political ſuperfluity or a
chaos of unknown things.

Some kind of official department, to which
reports ſhall be made from the different parts of
a nation, or from abroad, to be laid before the
national repreſentatives, is all that is neceſſary;
but there is no conſiſtency in calling this the
executive; neither can it be conſidered in any
other light than as inferior to the legiſlative.
The ſovereign authority in any country is the
power of making laws, and every thing elſe is an
official department.

Next to the arrangement of the principles and
the organization of the ſeveral parts of a conſtitution, is the proviſion to be made for the ſupport of the perſons to whom the nation ſhall
confide the adminiſtration of the conſtitutional
powers.

A nation can have no right to the time and
ſervices of any perſon at his own expence, whom
it may chuſe to employ or entruſt in any department whatever; neither can any reaſon be given
                                                    for

for making provifion for the fupport of any one part of a government and not for the other.

But, admitting that the honour of being entrufted with any part of a government is to be confidered a fufficient reward, it ought to be fo to every perfon alike. If the members of the legiſlature of any country are to ferve at their own expence, that which is called the executive, whether monarchical, or by any other name, ought to ferve in like manner. It is inconfiftent to pay the one, and accept the fervice of the other gratis.

In America, every department in the government is decently provided for; but no one is extravagantly paid. Every member of Congrefs, and of the affemblies, is allowed a fufficiency for his expences. Whereas in England, a moft prodigal provifion is made for the fupport of one part of the government, and none for the other, the confequence of which is, that the one is furniſhed with the means of corruption, and the other is put into the condition of being corrupted. Lefs than a fourth part of fuch expence, applied as it is in America, would remedy a great part of the corruption.

Another reform in the American conftitutions, is the exploding all oaths of perfonality. The oath of allegiance in America is to the nation only. The putting any individual as a figure for a nation is improper. The happinefs of a nation is the fuperior object, and therefore the intention

of

of an oath of allegiance ought not to be obscured by being figuratively taken, to, or in the name of, any person. The oath, called the civic oath, in France, viz. the " *nation, the law, and the king,*" is improper. If taken at all, it ought to be as in America, to the nation only. The law may or may not be good; but, in this place, it can have no other meaning, than as being conducive to the happiness of the nation, and therefore is included in it. The remainder of the oath is improper, on the ground, that all personal oaths ought to be abolished. They are the remains of tyranny on one part, and slavery on the other; and the name of the CREATOR ought not to be introduced to witness the degradation of his creation; or if taken, as is already mentioned, as figurative of the nation, it is in this place redundant. But whatever apology may be made for oaths at the first establishment of a government, they ought not to be permitted afterwards. If a government requires the support of oaths, it is a sign that it is not worth supporting, and ought not to be supported. Make government what it ought to be, and it will support itself.

To conclude this part of the subject:—One of the greatest improvements that has been made for the perpetual security and progress of constitutional liberty, is the provision which the new constitutions make for occasionally revising, altering, and amending them.

The principle upon which Mr. Burke formed his

his political creed, that " *of binding and controul-* " *ing posterity to the end of time, and of renouncing* " *and abdicating the rights of all posterity for* " *ever,*" is now become too detestable to be made a subject of debate; and, therefore, I pass it over with no other notice than exposing it.

Government is but now beginning to be known. Hitherto it has been the mere exercise of power, which forbad all effectual enquiry into rights, and grounded itself wholly on possession. While the enemy of liberty was its judge, the progress of its principles must have been small indeed.

The constitutions of America, and also that of France; have either affixed a period for their revision, or laid down the mode by which improvements shall be made. It is perhaps impossible to establish any thing that combines principles with opinions and practice, which the progress of circumstances, through a length of years, will not in some measure derange, or render inconsistent; and, therefore, to prevent inconveniences accumulating, till they discourage reformations or provoke revolutions, it is best to provide the means of regulating them as they occur The Rights of Man are the rights of all generations of men, and cannot be monopolized by any. That which is worth following, will be followed for the sake of its worth; and it is in this that its security lies, and not in any conditions with which it may be encumbered. When a man
leaves

leaves property to his heirs, he does not conneſt
it with an obligation that they ſhall accept it.
Why then ſhould we do otherwiſe with reſpeſt to
conſtitutions ?

The beſt conſtitution that could now be deviſed, conſiſtent with the condition of the preſent
moment, may be far ſhort of that excellence
which a few years may afford. There is a
morning of reaſon riſing upon man on the
ſubjeſt of government, that has not appeared
before. As the barbariſm of the preſent old
governments expires, the moral condition of
nations with reſpeſt to each other will be
changed. Man will not be brought up with the
ſavage idea of conſidering his ſpecies as his enemy,
becauſe the accident of birth gave the individuals
exiſtence in countries diſtinguiſhed by different
names ; and as conſtitutions have always ſome
relation to external as well as to domeſtic circum-
ſtances, the means of benefiting by every change,
foreign or domeſtic, ſhould be a part of every conſtitution.

We already ſee an alteration in the national
diſpoſition of England and France towards each
other, which, when we look back to only a few
years, is itſelf a revolution. Who could have
foreſeen, or who would have believed, that a
French National Aſſembly would ever have been
a popular toaſt in England, or that a friendly
alliance of the two nations ſhould become the
wiſh of either. It ſhews, that man, were he not
corrupted

corrupted by governments, is naturally the friend of man, and that human nature is not of itfelf vicious. That fpirit of jealoufy and ferocity, which the governments of the two countries infpired, and which they rendered fubfervient to the purpofe of taxation, is now yielding to the dictates of reafon, intereft, and humanity. The trade of courts is beginning to be underftood, and the affectation of myftery, with all the artificial forcery by which they impofed upon mankind, is on the decline. It has received its death-wound; and though it may linger, it will expire.

Government ought to be as much open to improvement as any thing which appertains to man, inftead of which it has been monopolized from age to age, by the moft ignorant and vicious of the human race. Need we any other proof of their wretched management, than the excefs of debts and taxes with which every nation groans, and the quarrels into which they have precipitated the world?

Juft emerging from fuch a barbarous condition, it is too foon to determine to what extent of improvement government may yet be carried. For what we can forefee, all Europe may form but one great republic, and man be free of the whole.

CHAP.

C H A P. V.

WAYS and MEANS of improving the condition of Europe, interſperſed with Miscellaneous Observations.

IN contemplating a ſubjeƈt that embraces with equatorial magnitude the whole region of humanity, it is impoſſible to confine the purſuit in one ſingle direƈtion. It takes ground on every charaƈter and condition that appertains to man, and blends the individual, the nation, and the world.

From a ſmall ſpark, kindled in America, a flame has ariſen, not to be extinguiſhed. Without conſuming, like the *Ultima Ratio Regum*, it winds its progreſs from nation to nation, and conquers by a ſilent operation. Man finds himſelf changed, he ſcarcely perceives how. He acquires a knowledge of his rights by attending juſtly to his intereſt, and diſcovers in the event that the ſtrength and powers of deſpotiſm conſiſt wholly in the fear of reſiſting it, and that, in order " *to be* " *free, it is ſufficient that he wills it.*"

Having in all the preceding parts of this work endeavoured to eſtabliſh a ſyſtem of principles as a baſis, on which governments ought to be ereƈted; I ſhall proceed in this, to the ways and means of rendering them into praƈtice. But in order to introduce this part of the ſubjeƈt with

more

more propriety, and ftronger effect, fome preliminary obfervations, deducible from, or connected
with, thofe principles, are neceffary.

Whatever the form or conftitution of government may be, it ought to have no other object
than the *general* happinefs. When, inftead of this,
it operates to create and encreafe wretchednefs in
any of the parts of fociety, it is on a wrong fyftem, and reformation is neceffary.

Cuftomary language has claffed the condition
of man under the two defcriptions of civilized and
uncivilized life. To the one it has afcribed felicity and affluence; to the other hardfhip and want.
But, however, our imagination may be impreffed
by painting and comparifon, it is neverthelefs
true, that a great portion of mankind, in what
are called civilized countries, are in a ftate of
poverty and wretchednefs, far below the condition of an Indian. I fpeak not of one country, but
of all. It is fo in England, it is fo all over Europe. Let us enquire into the caufe.

It lies not in any natural defect in the principles of civilization, but in preventing thofe
principles having an univerfal operation; the confequence of which is, a perpetual fyftem of war
and expence, that drains the country, and defeats
the general felicity of which civilization is capable.

All the European governments (France now
excepted) are conftructed not on the principle of
univerfal civilization, but on the reverfe of it
So far as thofe governments relate to each other,
                                    they

they are in the same condition as we conceive of
savage uncivilized life; they put themselves beyond the law as well of GOD as of man, and are,
with respect to principle and reciprocal conduct,
like so many individuals in a state of nature.

The inhabitants of every country, under the
civilization of laws, easily civilize together, but
governments being yet in an uncivilized state, and
almost continually at war, they pervert the abundance which civilized life produces to carry on
the uncivilized part to a greater extent. By thus
engrafting the barbarism of government upon the
internal civilization of a country, it draws from
the latter, and more especially from the poor, a
great portion of those earnings, which should be
applied to their own subsistence and comfort.—A-
part from all reflections of morality and philosophy,
it is a melancholy fact, that more than one-fourth
of the labour of mankind is annually consumed
by this barbarous system.

What has served to continue this evil, is the
pecuniary advantage, which all the governments of
Europe have found in keeping up this state of un-
civilization. It affords to them pretences for
power, and revenue, for which there would be
neither occasion nor apology, if the circle of civilization were rendered compleat. Civil government alone, or the government of laws, is not
productive of pretences for many taxes; it operates at home, directly under the eye of the country, and precludes the possibility of much imposi-
tion. But when the scene is laid in the unciviliz-

ed

ed contention of governments, the field of pretences is enlarged, and the country, being no longer a judge, is open to every impofition, which governments pleafe to act.

Not a thirtieth, fcarely a fortieth, part of the taxes which are raifed in England are either occafioned by, or applied to, the purpofes of civil government. It is not difficult to fee, that the whole which the actual government does in this refpect, is to enact laws, and that the country adminifters and executes them, at its own expence, by means of magiftrates, juries, feffions, and affize, over and above the taxes which it pays.

In this view of the cafe, we have two diftinct characters of government; the one the civil government, or the government of laws, which operates at home, the other the court or cabinet government, which operates abroad, on the rude plan of uncivilized life; the one attended with little charge, the other with boundlefs extravagance; and fo diftinct are the two, that if the latter were to fink, as it were by a fudden opening of the earth, and totally difappear, the former would not be deranged. It would ftill proceed, becaufe it is the common intereft of the nation that it fhould, and all the means are in practice.

Revolutions, then, have for their object, a change in the moral condition of governments, and with this change the burthen of public taxes will leffen, and civilization will be left to the enjoyment of that abundance, of which it is now deprived.

G   In

In contemplating the whole of this fubject, I extend my views into the department of commerce. In all my publications, where the matter would admit, I have been an advocate for commerce, becaufe I am a friend to its effects. It is a pacific fyftem, operating to cordialize mankind, by rendering nations, as well as individuals, ufeful to each other. As to mere theoretical reformation, I have never preached it up. The moft effectual procefs is that of improving the condition of man by means of his intereft; and it is on this ground that I take my ftand.

If commerce were permitted to act to the univerfal extent it is capable, it would extirpate the fyftem of war, and produce a revolution in the uncivilized ftate of governments. The invention of commerce has arifen fince thofe governments began, and is the greateft approach towards univerfal civilization, that has yet been made by any means not immediately flowing from moral principles.

Whatever has a tendency to promote the civil intercourfe of nations, by an exchange of benefits, is a fubject as worthy of philofophy as of politics. Commerce is no other than the traffic of two individuals, multiplied on a fcale of numbers; and by the fame rule that nature intended the intercourfe of two, fhe intended that of all. For this purpofe fhe has diftributed the materials of manufactures and commerce, in various and diftant parts of a nation and of the world; and as they cannot be procured by war fo cheaply or fo com-

modioufly

modioufly as by commerce, fhe has rendered the latter the means of extirpating the former.

As the two are nearly the oppofites of each other, confequently, the uncivilized ftate of European governments is injurious to commerce. Every kind of deftruction or embarraffment ferves to leffen the quantity, and it matters but little in what part of the commercial world the reduction begins. Like blood, it cannot be taken from any of the parts, without being taken from the whole mafs in circulation, and all partake of the lofs. When the ability in any nation to buy is deftroyed, it equally involves the feller. Could the government of England deftroy the commerce of all other nations, fhe would moft effectually ruin her own.

It is poffible that a nation may be the carrier for the world, but fhe cannot be the merchant. She cannot be the feller and the buyer of her own merchandize. The ability to buy muft refide out of herfelf; and, therefore, the profperity of any commercial nation is regulated by the profperity of the reft. If they are poor fhe cannot be rich, and her condition, be it what it may, is an index of the height of the commercial tide in other nations.

That the principles of commerce, and its univerfal operation may be underftood, without underftanding the practice, is a pofition that reafon will not deny; and it is on this ground only that I argue the fubject. It is one thing in the

G 2   counting-

counting-houfe, in the world it is another. With refpect to its operation it muft neceffarily be contemplated as a reciprocal thing; that only one half its powers refides within the nation, and that the whole is as effectually deftroyed by deftroying the half that refides without, as if the deftruction had been committed on that which is within; for neither can act without the other.

When in the laft, as well as in former wars, the commerce of England funk, it was becaufe the general quantity was leffened every where; and it now rifes, becaufe commerce is in a rifing ftate in every nation. If England, at this day, imports and exports more than at any former period, the nations with which fhe trades muft neceffarily do the fame; her imports are their exports, and *vice verfa.*

There can be no fuch thing as a nation flourifh-ing alone in commerce; fhe can only participate; and the deftruction of it in any part muft necef-farily affect all. When, therefore, governments are at war, the attack is made upon the common ftock of commerce, and the confequence is the fame as if each had attacked his own.

The prefent increafe of commerce is not to be attributed to minifters, or to any political con-trivances, but to its own natural operations in confequence of peace. The regular markets had been deftroyed, the channels of trade broken up, the high road of the feas infefted with robbers of every nation, and the attention of the world called to other objects. Thofe interruptions have ceafed,

5   and

and peace has reſtored the deranged condition of things to their proper order *.

It is worth remarking, that every nation reckons the balance of trade in its own favour; and therefore ſomething muſt be irregular in the common ideas upon this ſubjeſt.

The faſt, however, is true, according to what is called a balance; and it is from this cauſe that commerce is univerſally ſupported. Every nation feels the advantage, or it would abandon the praſtice : but the deception lies in the mode of making up the accounts, and in attributing what are called profits to a wrong cauſe.

Mr. Pitt has ſometimes amuſed himſelf, by ſhewing what he called a balance of trade from the cuſtom-houſe books. This mode of calculation, not only affords no rule that is true, but one that is falſe.

In the firſt place, Every cargo that departs from the cuſtom-houſe, appears on the books as an export; and, according to the cuſtom-houſe balance, the loſſes at ſea, and by foreign failures,

---

* In America, the increaſe of commerce is greater in proportion than in England. It is, at this time, at leaſt one half more than at any period prior to the revolution. The greateſt number of veſſels cleared out of the port of Philadelphia, before the commencement of the war, was between eight and nine hundred. In the year 1788, the number was upwards of twelve hundred. As the ſtate of Pennſylvania is eſtimated as an eighth part of the United States in population, the whole number of veſſels muſt now be nearly ten thouſand.

are

are all reckoned on the fide of profit, becaufe they appear as exports.

Secondly, Becaufe the importation by the fmuggling trade does not appear on the cuftom-houfe books, to arrange againft the exports.

No balance, therefore, as applying to fuperior advantages, can be drawn from thofe documents; and if we examine the natural operation of commerce, the idea is fallacious; and if true, would foon be injurious. The great fupport of commerce confifts in the balance being a level of benefits among all nations.

Two merchants of different nations trading together, will both become rich, and each makes the balance in his own favour; confequently, they do not get rich out of each other; and it is the fame with refpect to the nations in which they refide. The cafe muft be, that each nation muft get rich out of its own means, and increafes that riches by fomething which it procures from another in exchange.

If a merchant in England fends an article of Englifh manufacture abroad, which cofts him a fhilling at home, and imports fomething which fells for two, he makes a balance of one fhilling in his own favour: but this is not gained out of the foreign nation or the foreign merchant, for he alfo does the fame by the article he receives, and neither has a balance of advantage upon the other. The original value of the two articles in their prope countries were but two fhillings; but by
changing

changing their places, they acquire a new idea of value, equal to double what they had at first, and that increased value is equally divided.

There is no otherwise a balance on foreign than on domestic commerce. The merchants of London and Newcastle trade on the same principles, as if they resided in different nations, and make their balances in the same manner: yet London does not get rich out of Newcastle, any more than Newcastle out of London: but coals, the merchandize of Newcastle, have an additional value at London, and London merchandize has the same at Newcastle.

Though the principle of all commerce is the same, the domestic, in a national view, is the part the most beneficial; because the whole of the advantages, on both sides, rests within the nation; whereas, in foreign commerce, it is only a participation of one half.

The most unprofitable of all commerce is that connected with foreign dominion. To a few individuals it may be beneficial, merely because it is commerce; but to the nation it is a loss. The expence of maintaining dominion more than absorbs the profits of any trade. It does not increase the general quantity in the world, but operates to lessen it; and as a greater mass would be afloat by relinquishing dominion, the participation without the expence would be more valuable than a greater quantity with it

But it is impossible to engross commerce by
dominion;

dominion; and therefore it is ſtill more fallacious. It cannot exiſt in confined channels, and neceſſarily breaks out by regular or irregular means, that defeat the attempt; and to ſucceed would be ſtill worſe. France, ſince the revolution, has been more than indifferent as to foreign poſſeſſions; and other nations will become the ſame, when they inveſtigate the ſubject with reſpect to commerce.

To the expence of dominion is to be added that of navies, and when the amount of the two are ſubtracted from the profits of commerce, it will appear, that what is called the balance of trade, even admitting it to exiſt, is not enjoyed by the nation, but abſorbed by the government.

The idea of having navies for the protection of commerce is deluſive. It is putting the means of deſtruction for the means of protection. Commerce needs no other protection than the reciprocal intereſt which every nation feels in ſupporting it—it is common ſtock—it exiſts by a balance of advantages to all; and the only interruption it meets, is from the preſent uncivilized ſtate of governments, and which it is its common intereſt to reform *

---

* When I ſaw Mr. Pitt's mode of eſtimating the balance of trade, in one of his parliamentary ſpeeches, he appeared to me to know nothing of the nature and intereſt of commerce; and no man has more wantonly tortured it than himſelf. During a period of peace, it has been havocked with the calamities of war. Three times has it been thrown into ſtagnation, and the yeſſels unmaned by impreſſing, within leſs than four years of peace.

Quitting

Quitting this fubject, I now proceed to other matters.—As it is neceffary to include England in the profpect of a general reformation, it is proper to enquire into the defects of its government. It is only by each nation reforming its own, that the whole can be improved, and the full benefit of reformation enjoyed. Only partial advantages can flow from partial reforms.

France and England are the only two countries in Europe where a reformation in government could have fuccefsfully begun. The one fecure by the ocean, and the other by the immenfity of its internal ftrength, could defy the malignancy of foreign defpotifm. But it is with revolutions as with commerce, the advantages increafe by their becoming general, and double to either what each would receive alone.

As a new fyftem is now opening to the view of the world, the European courts are plotting to counteract it. Alliances, contrary to all former fyftems, are agitating, and a common intereft of courts is forming againft the common intereft of man. This combination draws a line that runs throughout Europe, and prefents a caufe fo entirely new, as to exclude all calculations from former circumftances. While defpotifm warred with defpotifm, man had no intereft in the conteft; but in a caufe that unites the foldier with the citizen, and nation with nation, the defpotifm of courts, though it feels the danger, and meditates revenge, is afraid to ftrike.

No

No queſtion has ariſen within the records of hiſtory that preſſed with the importance of the preſent.   It is not whether this or that party ſhall be in or out, or whig or tory; or high or low ſhall prevail; but whether man ſhall inherit his rights, and univerſal civilization take place? Whether the fruits of his labours ſhall be enjoyed by himſelf, or conſumed by the profligacy of governments? Whether robbery ſhall be baniſhed from courts, and wretchedneſs from countries?

When, in countries that are called civilized, we ſee age going to the workhouſe and youth to the gallows, ſomething muſt be wrong in the ſyſtem of government.   It would ſeem, by the exterior appearance of ſuch countries, that all was happineſs; but there lies hidden from the eye of common obſervation, a maſs of wretchedneſs that has ſcarcely any other chance, than to expire in poverty or infamy.   Its entrance into life is marked with the preſage of its fate; and until this is remedied, it is in vain to puniſh.

Civil government does not conſiſt in executions; but in making that proviſion for the inſtruction of youth, and the ſupport of age, as to exclude, as much as poſſible, profligacy from the one, and deſpair from the other.   Inſtead of this, the reſources of a country are laviſhed upon kings, upon courts, upon hirelings, impoſters, and proſtitutes; and even the poor themſelves, with all their wants upon them, are compelled to ſupport the fraud that oppreſſes them.

Why

Why is it, that fcarcely any are executed but the poor? The fact is a proof, among other things, of a wretchednefs in their condition. Bred up without morals, and caft upon the world without a profpect, they are the expofed facrifice of vice and legal barbarity. The millions that are fuperfluoufly wafted upon governments, are more than fufficient to reform thofe evils, and to benefit the condition of every man in a nation, not included within the purlieus of a court. This I hope to make appear in the progrefs of this work.

It is the nature of compaffion to affociate with misfortune. In taking up this fubject I feek no recompence—I fear no confequence. Fortified with that proud integrity, that difdains to triumph or to yield, I will advocate the Rights of Man.

It is to my advantage that I have ferved an apprenticefhip to life. I know the value of moral inftruction, and I have feen the danger of the contrary.

At an early period, little more than fixteen years of age, raw and adventurous, and heated with the falfe heroifm of a mafter * who had ferved in a man of war, I began the carver of my own fortune, and entered on board the Terrible, Privateer, Capt. Death. From this adventure I

* Rev. William Knowles, mafter of the grammar fchool of Thetford, in Norfolk.

was

was happily prevented by the affectionate and moral remonstrance of a good father, who, from his own habits of life, being of the Quaker profession, must begin to look upon me as lost. But the impression, much as it effected at the time, began to wear away, and I entered afterwards in the King of Prussia Privateer, Capt. Mendez, and went with her to sea. Yet, from such a beginning, and with all the inconvenience of early life against me, I am proud to say, that with a perseverance undismayed by difficulties, a disinterestednefs that compelled respect, I have not only contributed to raise a new empire in the world, founded on a new system of government, but I have arrived at an eminence in political literature, the most difficult of all lines to succeed and excel in, which aristocracy, with all its aids, has not been able to reach or to rival.

Knowing my own heart, and feeling myself, as I now do, superior to all the skirmish of party, the inveteracy of interested or mistaken opponents, I answer not to falsehood or abuse, but proceed to the defects of the English government *.

I begin with charters and corporations.

It

* Politics and self-interest have been so uniformly connected, that the world, from being so often deceived, has a right to be suspicious of public characters : but with regard to myself, I am perfectly easy on this head. I did not, at my first setting out in public life, nearly seventeen years ago, turn my thoughts to subjects of

It is a perverfion of terms to fay, that a charter gives rights. It operates by a contrary effect, that of taking rights away. Rights are inherently

in

of government from motives of intereft; and my conduct from that moment to this, proves the fact. I faw an opportunity, in which I thought I could do fome good, and I followed exactly what my heart dictated. I neither read books, nor ftudied other people's opinions. I thought for myfelf. The cafe was this:

During the fufpenfion of the old governments in America, both prior to, and at the breaking out of hoftilities, I was ftruck with the order and decorum with which every thing was conducted; and impreffed with the idea, that a little more than what fociety naturally performed, was all the government that was neceffary; and that monarchy and ariftocracy were frauds and impofitions upon mankind. On thefe principles I pub-lifhed the pamphlet *Common Senfe*. The fuccefs it met with was beyond any thing fince the invention of printing. I gave the copy right up to every ftate in the union, and the demand ran to not lefs than one hundred thoufand copies. I continued the fubject in the fame manner, under the title of the *Crifis*, till the complete eftablifhment of the revolution.

After the declaration of independence, Congrefs unani-moufly, and unknown to me, appointed me fecretary in the foreign department. This was agreeable to me, becaufe it gave me the opportunity of feeing into the abilities of foreign courts, and their manner of doing bufinefs. But a mifunderftanding arifing between congrefs and me, refpecting one of their com-miffioners, then in Europe, Mr. Silas Deane, I refigned the office, and declined, at the fame time, the pecuniary offers made me by the minifters of France and Spain, M. Gerard and Don Juan Mirralles.

I had by this time fo completely gained the ear and confi-dence of America, and my own independence was become fo vifible as to give me a range in political writing, beyond, per-haps, what any man ever poffeffed in any country; and what

is

in all the inhabitants; but charters, by annulling
thofe rights in the majority, leave the right by
exclufion

is more extraordinary, I held it undiminifhed to the end of the
war, and enjoy it in the fame manner to the prefent moment.
As my object was not myfelf, I fet out with the determination,
and happily with the difpofition, of not being moved by praife
or cenfure, friendfhip or calumny, nor of being drawn from my
purpofe by any perfonal altercation; and the man who cannot
do this, is not fit for a public character.

When the war ended, I went from Philadelphia to Borden-
Town, on the eaft bank of the Delaware, where I have a fmall
place. Congrefs was at this time at Prince-Town, fifteen
miles diftant; and General Wafhington had taken his head
quarters at Rocky-Hill, within the neighbourhood of Congrefs,
for the purpofe of refigning up his commiffion, (the object for
which he accepted it being accomplifhed,) and of retiring to
private life. While he was on this bufinefs, he wrote me the
letter which I here fubjoin.

Rocky-Hill, Sept. 10, 1783.
I have learned fince I have been at this place, that you are at
Borden-Town. Whether for the fake of retirement or œconomy, I know not. Be it for either, for both, or whatever it
may, if you will come to this place, and partake with me, I
fhall be exceedingly happy to fee yon at it.

Your prefence may remind Congrefs of your paft fervices to
this country; and if it is in my power to imprefs them, com-
mand my beft exertions with freedom, as they will be rendered
chearfully by one, who entertains a lively fenfe of the importance of your works, and who, with much pleafure, fubfcribes
himfelf,   Your fincere friend,
G. WASHINGTON.

During the war, in the latter end of the year 1780, I formed
to myfelf a defign of coming over to England; and communi-
cated it to General Greene, who was then in Philadelphia, on
his route to the fouthward, General Wafhington being then at
too

exclufion in the hands of a few.   If charters were
conftructed fo as to exprefs in direct terms,
                                    " *that*

too great a diftance to communicate with immediately. I was
ftrongly impreffed with the idea, that if I could get over to
England, without being known, and only remain in fafety till
I could get out a publication, that I could open the eyes of the
country with refpect to the madnefs and ftupidity of its government.   I faw that the parties in parliament had pitted themfelves as far as they could go, and could make no new impref-
fions on each other.   General Greene entered fully into my
views; but the affair of Arnold and André happening juft
after, he changed his mind, and, under ftrong apprehenfions
for my fafety, wrote very preffingly to me from Anapolis, in
Maryland, to give up the defign, which, with fome reluctance, I
did.   Soon after this I accompanied Col. Lawrens, fon of Mr.
Lawrens, who was then in the Tower, to France, on bufinefs
from Congrefs.   We landed at L'Orient; and while I remained
there, he being gone forward, a circumftance occurred, that
renewed my former defign.   An Englifh packet from Falmouth
to New-York, with the government difpatches on board, was
brought into L'Orient.   That a packet fhould be taken, is no
extraordinary thing; but that the difpatches fhould be taken
with it, will fcarcely be credited, as they are always flung at the
cabin window, in a bag loaded with cannon-ball, and ready to
be funk at a moment.   The fact, however, is as I have ftated
it, for the difpatches came into my hands, and I read them.
The capture, as I was informed, fucceeded by the following
ftratagem:—The captain of the Madame privateer, who fpoke
Englifh, on coming up with the packet, paffed himfelf for the
captain of an Englifh frigate, and invited the captain of the
packet on board, which, when done, he fent fome of his own
hands back, and fecured the mail.   But be the circumftance of
the capture what it may, I fpeak with certainty as to the
government difpatches.   They were fent up to Paris, to Count
Vergennes, and when Col. Lawrens and myfelf returned to
America, we took the originals to Congrefs.

                                                    By

" *that every inhabitant, who is not a member of a*
" *corporation, shall not exercise the right of voting,*"
such charters would, in the face, be charters, not
of rights, but of exclusion. The effect is the
same under the form they now stand; and the
only persons on whom they operate, are the
persons whom they exclude. Those whose rights
are guaranteed, by not being taken away, exercise no other rights, than as members of the community they are entitled to without a charter;
and, therefore, all charters have no other than an
indirect negative operation. They do not give
rights to A, but they make a difference in favour
of A by taking away the right of B, and confequently are instruments of injustice.

But charters and corporations have a more
extensive evil effect, than what relates merely to
elections. They are sources of endless contentions in the places where they exist; and they
lessen the common rights of national society. A
native of England, under the operation of these
charters and corporations, cannot be said to be
an Englishman in the full sense of the word.
He is not free of the nation, in the same manner

By these dispatches I saw into the stupidity of the English
cabinet, far more than I otherwise could have done, and I
renewed my former design.   But Col. Lawrens was so unwill-
ing to return alone ; more especially, as among other matters,
we had a charge of upwards of two hundred thousand pounds
sterling in money, that I gave into his wishes, and finally gave
up my plan.   But I am now certain, that if I could have executed it, that it would not have been altogether unsuccessful.

that

that a Frenchman is free of France, and an American of America. His rights are circumscribed to the town, and, in some cases, to the parish of his birth; and all other parts, though in his native land, are to him as a foreign country. To acquire a residence in these, he must undergo a local naturalization by purchase, or he is forbidden or expelled the place. This species of feudality is kept up to aggrandize the corporations at the ruin of towns; and the effect is visible.

The generality of corporation towns are in a state of solitary decay, and prevented from further ruin, only by some circumstance in their situation, such as a navigable river, or a plentiful surrounding country. As population is one of the chief sources of wealth, (for without it land itself has no value,) every thing which operates to prevent it must lessen the value of property; and as corporations have not only this tendency, but directly this effect, they cannot but be injurious. If any policy were to be followed, instead of that of general freedom, to every person to settle where he chose, (as in France or America,) it would be more consistent to give encouragement to new comers, than to preclude their admission by exacting premiums from them*.

The

---

* It is difficult to account for the origin of charter and corporation towns, unless we suppose them to have arisen out of, or been connected with, some species of garrison service. The

times

The perfons moft immediately interefted in the abolition of corporations, are the inhabitants of the towns where corporations are eftablifhed. The inftances of Manchefter, Birmingham, and Sheffield, fhew, by contraft, the injury which thofe Gothic inftitutions are to property and commerce. A few examples may be found, fuch as that of London, whofe natural and commercial advantage, owing to its fituation on the Thames, is capable of bearing up againft the political evils ·of a corporation ; but in almoft all other cafes the fatality is too vifible to be doubted or denied.

Though the whole nation is not fo directly affected by the depreffion of property in corporation towns as the inhabitants themfelves, it partakes of the confequence. By leffening the value of property, the quantity of national commerce is curtailed. Every man is a cuftomer in proportion to his ability ; and as all parts of a nation trade with each other, whatever affects any of

times in which they began juftify this idea. The generality of thofe towns have been garrifons ; and the corporations were charged with the care of the gates of the towns, when no military garrifon was prefent. Their refufing or granting admiffion to ftrangers, which has produced the cuftom of giving, felling, and buying freedom, has more of the nature of garrifon authority than civil government. Soldiers are free of all corporations throughout the nation, by the fame propriety that every foldier is free of every garrifon, and no other perfons are. He can follow any employment, with the permiffion of his officers, in any corporation town throughout the nation.

the

the parts, muſt neceſſarily communicate to the whole.

As one of the houſes of the Engliſh parliament is, in a great meaſure, made up of elections from theſe corporations; and as it is unnatural that a pure ſtream ſhould flow from a foul fountain, its vices are but a continuation of the vices of its origin. A man of moral honour and good political principles, cannot ſubmit to the mean drudgery and diſgraceful arts, by which ſuch elections are carried. To be a ſucceſsful candidate, he muſt be deſtitute of the qualities that conſtitute a juſt legiſlator: and being thus diſciplined to corruption by the mode of entering into parliament, it is not to be expected that the repreſentative ſhould be better than the man.

Mr. Burke, in ſpeaking of the Engliſh repreſentation, has advanced as bold a challenge as ever was given in the days of chivalry. "Our "repreſentation," ſays he, "has been found "*perfectly adequate to all the purpoſes* for which a "repreſentation of the people can be deſired or "deviſed. I defy," continues he, "the enemies "of our conſtitution to ſhew the contrary."——— This declaration from a man, who has been in conſtant oppoſition to all the meaſures of parliament the whole of his political life, a year or two excepted, is moſt extraordinary; and, comparing him with himſelf, admits of no other alternative, than that he acted againſt his judgment as a member, or has declared contrary to it as an author.

But

But it is not in the reprefentation only that the defects lie, and therefore I proceed in the next place to the ariftocracy.

What is called the Houfe of Peers, is confti-tuted on a ground very fimilar to that, againft which there is a law in other cafes. It amounts to a combination of perfons in one common intereft. No reafon can be given, why an houfe of legiflation fhould be compofed entirely of men whofe occupation confifts in letting landed pro-perty, than why it fhould be compofed of thofe who hire, or of brewers, or bakers, or any other feparate clafs of men.

Mr. Burke calls this houfe, *" the great ground " and pillar of fecurity to the landed intereft."* Let us examine this idea.

What pillar of fecurity does the landed intereft require more than any other intereft in the ftate, or what right has it to a diftinct and feparate reprefentation from the general intereft of a nation ? The only ufe to be made of this power, (and which it has always made,) is to ward off taxes from itfelf, and throw the burthen upon fuch articles of confumption by which itfelf would be leaft affected.

That this has been the confequence, (and will always be the confequence of conftructing govern-ments on combinations,) is evident with refpect to England, from the hiftory of its taxes.

Notwithftanding taxes have encreafed and mul-tiplied upon every article of common confumption,

tion, the land-tax, which more particularly affects this "pillar," has diminished. In 1788, the amount of the land-tax was 1,950,000£. which is half a million less than it produced almost an hundred years ago *, notwithstanding the rentals are in many instances doubled since that period.

Before the coming of the Hanoverians, the taxes were divided in nearly equal proportions between the land and articles of consumption, the land bearing rather the largest share: but since that æra, nearly thirteen millions annually of new taxes have been thrown upon consumption. The consequence of which has been a constant encrease in the number and wretchedness of the poor, and in the amount of the poor-rates. Yet here again the burthen does not fall in equal proportions on the aristocracy with the rest of the community. Their residences, whether in town or country, are not mixed with the habitations of the poor. They live apart from distress, and the expence of relieving it. It is in manufacturing towns and labouring villages that those burthens press the heaviest; in many of which it is one class of poor supporting another.

Several of the most heavy and productive taxes are so contrived, as to give an exemption to this pillar, thus standing in its own defence. The tax upon beer brewed for sale does not affect the ari-

---

* See Sir John Sinclair's History of the Revenue. The land-tax in 1646 was £2,473,499.

stocracy,

ftocracy, who brew their own beer free of this
duty.   It falls only on thofe who have not con-
veniency or ability to brew, and who muft purchafe it in fmall quantities.   But what will mankind think of the juftice of taxation, when they
know, that this tax alone, from which the ariftocracy are from circumftances exempt, is nearly
equal to the whole of the land-tax, being in the
year 1788, and it is not lefs now, 1,666,152£.
and with its proportion of the taxes on malt and
hops, it exceeds it.—That a fingle article, thus
partially confumed, and that chiefly by the working part, fhould be fubject to a tax, equal to that
on the whole rental of a nation, is, perhaps, a fact
not to be paralleled in the hiftories of revenues.

This is one of the confequences refulting from
an houfe of legiflation, compofed on the ground
of a combination of common intereft; for whatever their feparate politics as to parties may be,
in this they are united.   Whether a combination
acts to raife the price of any article for fale, or
the rate of wages; or whether it acts to throw
taxes from itfelf upon another clafs of the community, the principle and the effect are the fame;
and if the one be illegal, it will be difficult to
fhew that the other ought to exift.

It is to no ufe to fay, that taxes are firft propofed
in the houfe of commons; for as the other houfe
has always a negative, it can always defend itfelf;
and it would be ridiculous to fuppofe that its
acquiefcence in the meafures to be propofed were
not underftood before hand.   Befides which, it
has

has obtained fo much influence by borough-
traffic, and fo many of its relations and connections are diftributed on both fides of the commons, as to give it, befides an abfolute negative
in one houfe, a preponderancy in the other, in all
matters of common concern.

It is difficult to difcover what is meant by the
landed intereft, if it does not mean a combination
of ariftocratical land-holders, oppofing their own
pecuniary intereft to that of the farmer, and every
branch of trade, commerce, and manufacture.
In all other refpects it is the only intereft that
needs no partial protection. It enjoys the general
protection of the world. Every individual, high
or low, is interefted in the fruits of the earth;
men, women, and children, of all ages and
degrees, will turn out to affift the farmer, rather
than a harveft fhould not be got in; and they
will not act thus by any other property. It is the
only one for which the common prayer of mankind is put up, and the only one that can never
fail from the want of means. It is the intereft,
not of the policy, but of the exiftence of man,
and when it ceafes he muft ceafe to be.

No other intereft in a nation ftands on the
fame united fupport. Commerce, manufactures,
arts, fciences, and every thing elfe, compared
with this, are fupported but in parts. Their
profperity or their decay has not the fame univerfal influence. When the vallies laugh and

H 4   fing,

fing, it is not the farmer only, but all creation that rejoices. It is a profperity that excludes all envy; and this cannot be faid of any thing elfe.

Why then does Mr. Burke talk of his houfe of peers, as the pillar of the landed intereft? Were that pillar to fink into the earth, the fame landed property would continue, and the fame ploughing, fowing, and reaping would go on. The ariftocracy are not the farmers who work the land, and raife the produce, but are the mere confumers of the rent; and when compared with the active world, are the drones, a feraglio of males, who neither collect the honey nor form the hive, but exift only for lazy enjoyment.

Mr. Burke, in his firft effay, called ariftocracy, " *the Corinthian capital of polifhed fociety*." Towards compleating the figure, he has now added the *pillar*; but ftill the bafe is wanting; and whenever a nation chufes to act a Samfon, not blind, but bol , down go the temple of Dagon, the Lords and the Philiftines.

If a houfe of legiflation is to be compofed of men of one clafs, for the purpofe of protecting a diftinct intereft, all the other interefts fhould have the fame. The inequality, as well as the burthen of taxation, arifes from admitting it in one cafe, and not in all. Had there been an houfe of farmers, there had been no game laws; or an houfe of merchants and manuracturers, the taxes had neither been fo unequal nor fo exceffive. It is from the power of taxation being in
the

the hands of thofe who can throw fo great a part of it from their own fhoulders, that it has raged without a check.

Men of fmall or moderate eftates, are more injured by the taxes being thrown on articles of confumption, than they are eafed by warding it from landed property, for the following reafons:

Firft, They confume more of the productive taxable articles, in proportion to their property, than thofe of large eftates.

Secondly, Their refidence is chiefly in towns, and their property in houfes; and the encreafe of the poor-rates, occafioned by taxes on confumption, is in much greater proportion than the land-tax has been favoured. In Birmingham, the poor-rates are not lefs than feven fhillings in the pound. From this, as is already obferved, the ariftocracy are in a great meafure exempt.

Thefe are but a part of the mifchiefs flowing from the wretched fcheme of an houfe of peers.

As a combination, it can always throw a con-fiderable portion of taxes from itfelf; and as an hereditary houfe, accountable to nobody, it refembles a rotten borough, whofe confent is to be courted by intereft. There are but few of its members, who are not in fome mode or other participaters, or difpofers of the public money. One turns a candle-holder, or a lord in waiting; another a lord of the bed-chamber, a groom of the ftole, or any infignificant nominal office, to which a falary is annexed, paid out of the public

taxes,

taxes, and which avoids the direct appearance of corruption. Such fituations are derogatory to the character of man ; and where they can be fubmitted to, honour cannot refide.

To all thefe are to be added the numerous dependants, the long lift of younger branches and diftant relations, who are to be provided for at the public expence : in fhort, were an eftimation to be made of the charge of ariftocracy to a nation, it will be found nearly equal to that of fupporting the poor. The Duke of Richmond alone (and there are cafes fimilar to his) takes away as much for himfelf as would maintain two thoufand poor and aged perfons. Is it, then, any wonder, that under fuch a fyftem of government, taxes and rates have multiplied to their prefent extent ?

In ftating thefe matters, I fpeak an open and difinterefted language, dictated by no paffion but that of humanity. To me, who have not only refufed offers, becaufe I thought them improper, but have declined rewards I might with reputation have accepted, it is no wonder that meannefs and impofition appear difguftful. Independence is my happinefs, and I view things as they are, without regard to place or perfon ; my country is the world, and my religion is to do good.

Mr. Burke, in fpeaking of the ariftocratical law of primogeniture, fays, " it is the ftanding " law of our landed inheritance; and which, " without queftion, has a tendency, and I think,"

continues

continues he, " a happy tendency, to preferve a
" character of weight and confequence."

Mr. Burke may call this law what he pleafes,
but humanity and impartial reflection will de-
nounce it a law of brutal injuftice.   Were we not
accuftomed to the daily practice, and did we only
hear of it as the law of fome diftant part of the
world, we fhould conclude that the legiflators of
fuch countries had not yet arrived at a ftate of
civilization.

As to its preferving a character of *weight and
confequence*, the cafe appears to me directly the
reverfe.   It is an attaint upon character; a fort of
privateering on family property.   It may have
weight among dependent tenants, but it gives
none on a fcale of national, and, much lefs of
univerfal character.   Speaking for myfelf, my
parents were not able to give me a fhilling,
beyond what they gave me in education; and to
do this they diftreffed themfelves: yet, I poffefs
more of what is called confequence, in the world,
than any one in Mr. Burke's catalogue of ari_
ftocrats.

Having thus glanced at fome of the defects of
the two houfes of parliament, I proceed to what
is called the crown upon which I fhall be very
concife.

It fignifies a nominal office of a million fterling
a year, the bufinefs of which confifts in receiving.
the money.   Whether the perfon be wife or
foolifh, fane or infane, a native or a foreigner,
matters not.   Every miniftry acts upon the fame
idea

idea that Mr. Burke writes, namely, that the people muſt be hood-winked, and held in ſuperſtitious ignorance by ſome bugbear or other; and what is called the crown anſwers this purpoſe, and therefore it anſwers all the purpoſes to be expected from it. This is more than can be ſaid of the other two branches.

The hazard to which this office is expoſed in all countries, is not from any thing that can happen to the man, but from what may happen to the nation—the danger of its coming to its ſenſes.

It has been cuſtomary to call the crown the executive power, and the cuſtom is continued, though the reaſon has ceaſed.

It was called the *executive*, becauſe the perſon whom it ſignified uſed, formerly, to ſit in the character of a judge, in adminiſtering or executing the laws. The tribunals were then a part of the court. The power, therefore, which is now called the judicial, is what was called the execu. tive; and, conſequently, one or other of the terms is redundant, and one of the offices uſeleſs. When we ſpeak of the crown now, it means nothing; it ſignifies neither a judge nor a general: beſides which it is the laws that govern, and not the man. The old terms are kept up, to give an appearance of conſequence to empty forms; and the only effect they have is that of increaſing expences.

Before I proceed to the means of rendering governments more conducive to the general happineſs

happineſs of mankind, than they are at preſent, it will not be improper to take a review of the progreſs of taxation in England.

It is a general idea, that when taxes are once laid on, they are never taken off. However true this may have been of late, it was not always ſo. Either, therefore, the people of former times were more watchful over government than thoſe of the preſent, or government was adminiſtered with leſs extravagance.

It is now ſeven hundred years ſince the Norman conqueſt, and the eſtabliſhment of what is called the crown. Taking this portion of time in ſeven ſeparate periods of one hundred years each, the amount of the annual taxes, at each period, will be as follows:—

Annual amount of taxes levied by William the Conqueror, beginning in the year 1066, — — £. 400,000

Annual amount of taxes at one hundred years from the conqueſt, (1166) ———— ———— 200,000

Annual amount of taxes at two hundred years from the conqueſt, (1266) ——— ———— 150,000

Annual amount of taxes at three hundred years from the conqueſt, (1366) ——— ———— 130,000

Annual amount of taxes at four hundred years from the conqueſt, (1466) ——— ———— 100,000

Theſe

These statements, and those which follow, are taken from Sir John Sinclair's History of the Revenue; by which it appears, that taxes continued decreasing for four hundred years, at the expiration of which time they were reduced three-fourths, viz. from four hundred thousand pounds to one hundred thousand. The people of England of the present day, have a traditionary and historical idea of the bravery of their ancestors; but whatever their virtues or their vices might have been, they certainly were a people who would not be imposed upon, and who kept government in awe as to taxation, if not as to principle. Though they were not able to expel the monarchical usurpation, they restricted it to a republican œconomy of taxes.

Let us now review the remaining three hundred years.

Annual amount of taxes at five hundred years from the conquest, (1566) — —	£.500,000
Annual amount of taxes at six hundred years from the conquest, (1666) — —	1,800,000
Annual amount of taxes at the present time, (1791) ——	17,000,000

The difference between the first four hundred years and the last three, is so astonishing, as to warrant an opinion, that the national character of the English has changed. It would have been

2   impossible

impoſſible to have dragooned the former Engliſh, into the exceſs of taxation that now exiſts; and when it is conſidered that the pay of the army, the navy, and of all the revenue-officers, is the ſame now as it was above a hundred years ago, when the taxes were not above a tenth part of what they are at preſent, it appears impoſſible to account for the enormous increaſe and expenditure, on any other ground, than extravagance, corruption, and intrigue *.

With

---

* Several of the court newſpapers have of late made frequent mention of Wat Tyler. That his memory ſhould be traduced by court ſycophants, and all thoſe who live on the ſpoil of a public, is not to be wondered at. He was, however, the means of checking the rage and injuſtice of taxation in his time, and the nation owed much to his valour. The hiſtory is conciſely this:—In the time of Richard the ſecond, a poll-tax was levied, of one ſhilling per head, upon every perſon in the nation, of whatever eſtate or condition, on poor as well as rich, above the age of fifteen years. If any favour was ſhewn in the law, it was to the rich rather than to the poor; as no perſon could be charged more than twenty ſhillings for himſelf, family, and ſervants, though ever ſo numerous; while all other families, under the number of twenty, were charged per head. Poll-taxes had always been odious; but this being alſo oppreſ-five and unjuſt, it excited, as it naturally muſt, univerſal deteſ-tation among the poor and middle claſſes. The perſon known by the name of Wat Tyler, whoſe proper name was Walter, and a tyler by trade, lived at Deptford. The gatherer of the poll-tax, on coming to his houſe, demanded tax for one of his daughters, whom Tyler declared was under the age of fifteen. The tax-gatherer inſiſted on ſatisfying himſelf, and began an indecent examination of the girl, which enraging the father, he ſtruck him with a hammer, that brought him to the ground, and was the cauſe of his death.

This

With the revolution of 1688, and more so
since the Hanover succession, came the destruc-
tive system of continental intrigues, and the rage
for foreign wars and foreign dominion; systems
of such secure mystery that the expences admit
of no accounts; a single line stands for millions.
To what excess taxation might have extended,
had not the French revolution contributed to
break up the system, and put an end to pretences,
is impossible to say. Viewed, as that revolution
ought to be, as the fortunate means of lessening
the load of taxes of both countries, it is of as

This circumstance served to bring the discontents to an issue.
The inhabitants of the neighbourhood espoused the cause of
Tyler, who, in a few days was joined, according to some histories,
by upwards of fifty thousand men, and chosen their chief. With
this force he marched to London, to demand an abolition of
the tax, and a redress of other grievances. The court, finding
itself in a forlorn condition, and unable to make resistance,
agreed, with Richard at its head, to hold a conference with
Tyler in Smithfield, making many fair professions, courtier
like, of its dispositions to redress the oppressions. While
Richard and Tyler were in conversation on these matters, each
being on horseback, Walworth, then mayor of London, and
one of the creatures of the court, watched an opportunity, and
like a cowardly assassin, stabbed Tyler with a dagger; and two
or three others falling upon him, he was instantly sacrificed.
Tyler appears to have been an intrepid disinterested man,
with respect to himself. All his proposals made to Richard,
were on a more just and public ground, than those which had
been made to John by the Barons; and notwithstanding the
sycophancy of historians, and men like Mr. Burke, who seek
to gloss over a base action of the court by traducing Tyler, his
fame will outlive their falsehood. If the Barons merited a
monument to be erected in Runnymede, Tyler merits one in
Smithfield.

much

much importance to England as to France; and, if properly improved to all the advantages of which it is capable, and to which it leads, deferve as much celebration in one country as the other.

In purfuing this fubjeft, I fhall begin with the matter that firft prefents itfelf, that of leffening the burthen of taxes; and fhall then add fuch matters and propofitions, refpecting the three countries of England, France, and America, as the prefent profpect of things appears to juftify: I mean, an alliance of the three, for the purpofes that will be mentioned in their proper place.

What has happened may happen again. By the ftatement before fhewn of the progrefs of taxation, it is feen, that taxes have been leffened to a fourth part of what they had formerly been. Though the prefent circumftances do not admit of the fame reduction, yet it admits of fuch a beginning, as may accomplifh that end in lefs time, than in the former cafe.

The amount of taxes for the year, ending at Michaelmas 1788, was as follows:

Land-tax, - -	£ 1,950,000
Cuftoms, - -	3,789,274
Excife, (including old and new malt,)	6,751,727
Stamps, - -	1,278,214
Mifcellaneous taxes and incidents,	1,803,755

£ 15,572,970

Since

Since the year 1788, upwards of one million, new taxes, have been laid on, befides the produce from the lotteries; and as the taxes have in general been more productive fince than before, the amount may be taken, in round numbers, at

£ 17,000,000

N. B. The expence of collection and the draw-backs, which together amount to nearly two millions, are paid out of the grofs amount; and the above is the nett fum paid into the exchequer.

This fum of feventeen millions is applied to two different purpofes; the one to pay the intereft of the national debt, the other to the current ex-pences of each year. About nine millions are ap-propriated to the former; and the remainder, being nearly eight millions, to the latter. As to the million, faid to be applied to the reduction of the debt, it is fo much like paying with one hand and taking out with the other, as not to merit much notice.

It happened, fortunately for France, that fhe poffeffed national domains for paying off her debt, and thereby leffening her taxes: but as this is not the cafe in England, her reduction of taxes can only take place by reducing the current expences, which may now be done to the amount of four or five millions annually, as will hereafter appear. When this is accomplifhed, it will more than counterbalance the enormous charge of the American war; and the faving will

4   be

be from the same source from whence the evil arose.

As to the national debt, however heavy the interest may be in taxes; yet, as it serves to keep alive a capital, useful to commerce, it balances by its effects a considerable part of its own weight; and as the quantity of gold and silver in England is, by some means or other, short of its proper proportion *, (being not more than twenty millions, whereas it should be sixty,) it would, besides the injustice, be bad policy to extinguish a capital that serves to supply that defect. But with respect to the current expence, whatever is saved therefrom is gain. The excess may serve to keep corruption alive, but it has no re-action on credit and commerce, like the interest of the debt.

It is now very probable, that the English government (I do not mean the nation) is unfriendly to the French revolution. Whatever serves to expose the intrigue and lessen the influence of courts, by lessening taxation, will be unwelcome to those who feed upon the spoil. Whilst the clamour of French intrigue, arbitrary power, popery, and wooden shoes could be kept up, the nation was easily allured and alarmed into taxes. Those days are now past; deception, it is to be hoped, has reaped its last harvest, and better times are in prospect for both countries, and for the world.

* Foreign intrigue, foreign wars, and foreign dominions, will in a great measure account for the deficiency.

Taking

Taking it for granted, that an alliance may be formed between England, France, and America, for the purposes hereafter to be mentioned, the national expences of France and England may consequently be leſſened. The ſame fleets and armies will no longer be neceſſary to either, and the reduction can be made ſhip for ſhip on each ſide. But to accompliſh theſe objects, the governments muſt neceſſarily be fitted to a common and correſpondent principle. Confidence can never take place, while an hoſtile diſpoſition remains in either, or where myſtery and ſecrecy on one ſide, is oppoſed to candour and openneſs on the other.

Theſe matters admitted, the national expences might be put back, *for the ſake of a precedent,* to what they were at ſome period when France and England were not enemies. This, conſequently, muſt be prior to the Hanover ſucceſſion, and alſo to the revolution of 1688 *. The firſt inſtance

that

---

* I happened to be in England at the celebration of the centenary of the revolution of 1688. The characters of William and Mary have always appeared to me deteſtable; the one ſeeking to deſtroy his uncle, and the other her father, to get poſſeſſion of power themſelves; yet, as the nation was diſpoſed to think ſomething of that event, I felt hurt at ſeeing it aſcribe the whole reputation of it to a man who had undertaken it as a jobb, and who beſides what he otherwiſe got, charged ſix hundred thouſand pounds for the expence of the little fleet that brought him from Holland. George the Firſt acted the ſame cloſe-fiſted part as William had done, and bought the Duchy of Bremin with the money he got from England, two

hundred

that prefents itfelf, antecedent to thofe dates, is in the very wafteful and profligate times of Charles the Second; at which time England and France acted as allies. If I have chofen a period of great extravagance, it will ferve to fhew modern extravagance in a ftill worfe light; efpecially as the pay of the navy, the army, and the revenue officers has not encreafed fince that time.

The peace eftablifhment was then as follows:— See Sir John Sinclair's Hiftory of the Revenue.

Navy,	-	-	300,000
Army,	-	-	212,000
Ordnance,	-	-	40,000
Civil Lift,	-	-	462,115

£ 1,014,115

The parliament, however, fettled the whole annual peace eftablifhment at 1,200,000 *. If we go back to the time of Elizabeth, the amount

hundred and fifty thoufand pounds over and above his pay as king; and having thus purchafed it at the expence of England, added it to his Hanoverian dominions for his own private profit. In fact, every nation that does not govern itfelf, is governed as a jobb. England has been the prey of jobbs ever fince the revolution.

* Charles, like his predeceffors and fucceffors, finding that war was the harveft of governments, engaged in a war with the Dutch, the expence of which encreafed the annual expenditure to £ 1,800,000, as ftated under the date of 1666; but the peace eftablifhment was but £ 1,200,000.

of

of all the taxes was but half a million, yet the nation fees nothing during that period, that reproaches it with want of confequence.

All circumftances then taken together, arifing from the French revolution, from the approaching harmony and reciprocal intereft of the two nations, the abolition of court intrigue on both fides, and the progrefs of knowledge in the fcience of government, the annual expenditure might be put back to one million and an half, viz.

Navy,	—	—	500,000
Army,	—	—	500,000
Expences of government,			500,000

£. 1,500,000

Even this fum is fix times greater than the expences of government are in America, yet the civil internal government in England, (I mean that adminiftered by means of quarter feffions, juries, and affize, and which, in fact, is nearly the whole, and performed by the nation,) is lefs expence upon the revenue, than the fame fpecies and portion of government is in America.

It is time that nations fhould be rational, and not be governed like animals, for the pleafure of their riders. To read the hiftory of kings, a man would be almoft inclined to fuppofe that government confifted in ftag-hunting, and that every nation paid a million a year to a huntfman. Man ought to have pride, or fhame enough to blufh at being thus impofed upon, and when he

feel

feel his proper character, he will.   Upon all fubjects of this nature, there is often paffing in
the mind, a train of ideas he has not yet accuftomed
himfelf to encourage and communicate.   Re-
ftrained by fomething that puts on the character
of prudence, he acts the hypocrite upon himfelf
as well as to others.   It is, however, curious to
obferve how foon this fpell can be diffolved.   A
fingle expreffion, boldly conceived and uttered,
will fometimes put a whole company into their
proper feelings; and whole nations are acted upon
in the fame manner.

As to the offices of which any civil government
may be compofed, it matters but little by what
names they are defcribed.   In the rotine of bufinefs, as before obferved, whether a man be ftiled
a prefident, a king, an emperor, a fenator, or any
thing elfe, it is impoffible that any fervice he can
perform, can merit from a nation more than ten
thoufand pounds a year; and as no man fhould be
paid beyond his fervices, fo every man of a proper
heart will not accept more.   Public money ought
to be touched with the moft fcrupulous confciouf-
nefs of honour.   It is not the produce of riches
only, but of the hard earnings of labour and
poverty.   It·is drawn even from the bitternefs of
want and mifery.   Not a beggar paffes, or perifhes
in the ftreets, whofe mite is not in that mafs.

Were it poffible that the Congrefs of America,
could be fo loft to their duty, and to the intereft
of their conftituents, as to offer General Wafhing-

I 4   ton,

ton, as prefident of America, a million a year, he would not, and he could not, accept it. His fenfe of honour is of another kind. It has coft England almoft feventy millions fterling, to maintain a family imported from abroad, of very inferior capacity to thoufands in the nation; and fcarcely a year has paffed that has not produced fome new mercenary application. Even the phyficians bills have been fent to the public to be paid. No wonder that jails are crowded, and taxes and poor-rates encreafed. Under fuch fyftems, nothing is to be looked for but what has already happened; and as to reformation, whenever it come, it muft be from the nation, and not from the goverment.

To fhew that the fum of five hundred thoufand pounds is more than fufficient to defray all the expences of government, exclufive of navies and armies, the following eftimate is added for any country, of the fame extent as England.

In the firft place, three hundred reprefentatives, fairly elected, are fufficient for all the purpofes to which legiflation can apply, and preferable to a larger number. They may be divided into two or three houfes, or meet in one, as in France, or in any manner a conftitution fhall direct.

As reprefentation is always confidered, in free countries, as the moft honourable of all ftations, the allowance made to it is merely to defray the expence which the reprefentatives incur by that fervice, and not to it as an office.

If

If an allowance, at the rate of five ⎤
hundred pounds *per ann.* be made ⎟
to every reprefentative, deducting ⎟
for non-attendance, the expence, ⎬ £. 75,000
if the whole number attended for ⎟
fix months, each year, would be ⎦

The official departments cannot reafonably exceed the following number, with the falaries annexed:

Three offices, at ten thoufand pounds each 30,000
Ten   ditto,   at £. 5000 each   50,000
Twenty ditto,   at £. 2000 each   40,000
Forty   ditto,   at £. 1000 each   40,000
Two hundred ditto,   at £. 500 each 100,000
Three hundred ditto,   at £. 200 each   60,000
Five hundred ditto,   at £. 100 each   50,000
Seven hundred ditto,   at £.   75 each   52,500

£. 497,500

If a nation chufe, it can deduct four *per cent.* from all offices, and make one of twenty thoufand *per ann.*

All revenue officers are paid out of the monies they collect, and therefore, are not in this eftimation.

The foregoing is not offered as an exact detail of offices, but to fhew the number and rate of falaries which five hundred thoufand pounds will fupport; and it will, on experience, be found impracticable to find bufinefs fufficient to juftify even this expence. As to the manner in which

office.

office bufinefs is now performed, the Chiefs, in feveral offices, fuch as the poft-office, and certain offices in the exchequer, &c. do little more than fign their names three or four times a year; and the whole duty is performed by under clerks.

Taking, therefore, one million and an half as a fufficient peace eftablifhment for all the honeft purpofes of government, which is three hundred thoufand pounds more than the peace eftablifhment in the profligate and prodigal times of Charles the Second, (notwithftanding, as has been already obferved, the pay and falaries of the army, navy, and revenue officers, continue the fame as at that period,) there will remain a furplus of upwards of fix millions out of the prefent current expences. The queftion then will be, how to difpofe of this furplus.

Whoever has obferved the manner in which trade and taxes twift themfelves together, muft be fenfible of the impoffibility of feparating them fuddenly.

Firft. Becaufe the articles now on hand are already charged with the duty, and the reduction cannot take place on the prefent ftock.

Secondly. Becaufe, on all thofe articles on which the duty is charged in the grofs, fuch as *per* barrel, hogfhead, hundred weight, or tun, the abolition of the duty does not admit of being divided down fo as fully to relieve the confumer, who purchafes by the pint, or the pound. The laft duty laid on ftrong beer and ale, was three
fhillings

fhillings *per* barrel, which, if taken off, would leffen the purchafe only half a farthing *per* pint, and confequently, would not reach to practical relief.

This being the condition of a great part of the taxes, it will be neceffary to look for fuch others as are free from this embarraffment, and where the relief will be direct and vifible, and capable of immediate operation.

In the firft place, then, the poor-rates are a direct tax which every houfe-keeper feels, and who knows alfo, to a farthing, the fum which he pays. The national amount of the whole of the poor rates is not pofitively known, but can be procured. Sir John Sinclair, in his Hiftory of the Revenue, has ftated it at £. 2,100,587. A confiderable part of which is expended in litigations, in which the poor, inftead of being relieved, are tormented. The expence, however, is the fame to the parifh from whatever caufe it arifes.

In Birmingham, the amount of the poor-rates is fourteen thoufand pounds a year. This, though a large fum, is moderate, compared with the population. Birmingham is faid to contain feventy thoufand fouls, and on a proportion of feventy thoufand to fourteen thoufand pounds poor-rates, the national amount of poor-rates, taking the population of England at feven millions, would be but one million four hundred thoufand pounds. It is, therefore, moft probable, that the population of Birmingham is over-rated.

Fourteen

Fourteen thoufand pounds is the proportion upon fifty thoufand fouls, taking two millions of poor-rates as the national amount.

Be it, however, what it may, it is no other than the confequence of the exceffive burthen of taxes, for, at the time when the taxes were very low, the poor were able to maintain themfelves; and there were no poor-rates *. In the prefent ftate of things, a labouring man, with a wife and two or three children, does not pay lefs than between feven and eight pounds a year in taxes. He is not fenfible of this, becaufe it is difguifed to him in the articles which he buys, and he thinks only of their dearnefs; but as the taxes take from him, at leaft, a fourth part of his yearly earnings, he is confequently difabled from providing for a family, efpecially, if himfelf, or any of them, are afflicted with ficknefs.

The firft ftep, therefore, of practical relief, would be to abolifh the poor-rates entirely, and in lieu thereof, to make a remiffion of taxes to the poor of double the amount of the prefent poor-rates, viz. four millions annually out of the furplus taxes. By this meafure, the poor would be benefited two millions, and the houfe-keepers two millions. This alone would be equal to a reduction of one hundred and twenty millions of the national

---

* Poor-rates began about the time of Henry the Eighth, when the taxes began to encreafe, and they have encreafed as the taxes encreafed ever fince.

debt,

debt, and confequently equal to the whole expence of the American war.

It will then remain to be confidered, which is the moft effectual mode of diftributing this remif-fion of four millions.

It is eafily feen, that the poor are generally compofed of large families of children, and old people paft their labour. If thefe two claffes are provided for, the remedy will fo far reach to the full extent of the cafe, that what remains will be incidental, and, in a great meafure, fall within the compafs of benefit clubs, which, though of hum-ble invention, merit to be ranked among the beft of modern inftitutions.

Admitting England to contain feven million of fouls; if one-fifth thereof are of that clafs of poor which need fupport, the number will be one mil-lion four hundred thoufand. Of this number, one hundred and forty thoufand will be aged poor, as will be hereafter fhewn, and for which a diftinct provifion will be propofed.

There will then remain one million two hun-dred and fixty thoufand, which, at five fouls to each family, amount to two hundred and fifty-two thoufand families, rendered poor from the ex-pence of children and the weight of taxes.

The number of children under fourteen years of age, in each of thofe families, will be found to be about five to every two families; fome having two, and others three; fome one, and others four; fome none, and others five; but it rarely happens
that

that more than five are under fourteen years of age, and after this age they are capable of service or of being apprenticed.

Allowing five children (under fourteen years) to every two families,

The number of children will be   -   630,000
The number of parents were they all living, would be   -   -   504,000

It is certain, that if the children are provided for, the parents are relieved of consequence, because it is from the expence of bringing up children that their poverty arises.

Having thus ascertained the greatest number that can be supposed to need support on account of young families, I proceed to the mode of relief or distribution, which is,

To pay as a remission of taxes to every poor family, out of the surplus taxes, and in room of poor-rates, four pounds a year for every child under fourteen years of age; enjoining the parents of such children to send them to school, to learn reading, writing, and common arithmetic; the ministers of every parish, of every denomination, to certify jointly to an office, for that purpose, that this duty is performed.

The amount of this expence will be,
For six hundred and thirty thousand children, at four pounds, *per ann.* each,   £.2,520,000

By adopting this method, not only the poverty of the parents will be relieved. but ignorance will be banished from the rising generation, and the
number

number of poor will hereafter become lefs, becaufe their abilities, by the aid of education, will be greater. Many a youth, with good natural genius, who is apprenticed to a mechanical trade, fuch as a carpenter, joiner, millwright, fhipwright, black-fmith, &c. is prevented getting forward the whole of his life, from the want of a little common education when a boy.

I now proceed to the cafe of the aged.

I divide age into two claffes. Firft, the approach of age beginning at fifty. Secondly, old age commencing at fixty.

At fifty, though the mental faculties of man are in full vigour, and his judgment better than at any preceeding date, the bodily powers for laborious life are on the decline. He cannot bear the fame quantity of fatigue as at an earlier period. He begins to earn lefs, and is lefs capable of enduring wind and weather; and in thofe more retired employments where much fight is required, he fails apace, and fees himfelf, like an old horfe, beginning to be turned adrift.

At fixty his labour ought to be over, at leaft from direct neceffity. It is painful to fee old age working itfelf to death, in what are called civilized countries, for daily bread.

To form fome judgment of the number of thofe above fifty years of age, I have feveral times counted the perfons I met in the ftreets of London, men, women, and children, and have generally found that the average is about one in fixteen or feventeen.

feventeen. If it be faid that aged perfons do not come much in the ftreets, fo neither do infants; and a great proportion of grown children are in fchools, and in work fhops as apprentices. Taking then fixteen for a divifor, the whole number of perfons, in England, of fifty years and upwards of both fexes, rich and poor, will be four hundred and twenty thoufand.

The perfons to be provided for out of this grofs number will be, hufbandmen, common labourers, journeymen of every trade and their wives, failors, and difbanded foldiers, worn out fervants of both fexes, and poor widows.

There will be alfo a confiderable number of middling tradefmen, who having lived decently in the former part of life, begin, as age approaches, to lofe their bufinefs, and at laft fall to decay.

Befides thefe, there will be conftantly thrown off from the revolutions of that wheel, which no man can ftop, nor regulate, a number from every clafs of life connected with commerce and adventure.

To provide for all thofe accidents, and whatever elfe may befal, I take the number of perfons, who at one time or other of their lives, after fifty years of age, may feel it neceffary or comfortable to be better fupported, than they can fupport themfelves, and that not as a matter of grace and favour, but of right, at one third of the whole number, which is one hundred and forty thoufand, as ftated in page 125, and for whom a diftinct provifion was propofed to be made. If there be
more

more, fociety, notwithftanding the fhew and pom-
pofity of government, is in a deplorable condition
in England.

Of this one hundred and forty thoufand, I take
one half, feventy thoufand, to be of the age of fifty
and under fixty, and the other half to be fixty
years and upwards.—Having thus afcertained the
probable proportion of the number of aged perfons, I proceed to the mode of rendering their
condition comfortable, which is,

To pay to every fuch perfon of the age of fifty
years, and until he fhall arrive at the age of fixty,
the fum of fix pounds *per ann.* out of the furplus
taxes; and ten pounds *per ann.* during life after
the age of fixty.   The expence of which will be,

Seventy thoufand perfons at £.6 *per ann.* 420,000
Seventy thoufand ditto   at £.10 *per ann.* 700,000
                                            ─────────
                              £. 1,120,000

This fupport, as already remarked, is not of
the nature of a charity, but of a right. Every
perfon in England, male and female, pays on an
average in taxes, two pounds eight fhillings and
fixpence *per ann.* from the day of his (or her)
birth; and, if the expence of collection be added, he
pays two pounds eleven fhillings and fixpence; confequently, at the end of fifty years he has paid one
hundred and twenty-eight pounds fifteen fhillings;
and at fixty, one hundred and fifty-four pounds ten
fhillings.   Converting, therefore, his (or her) in-

K   dividual

dividual tax into a tontine, the money he shall receive after fifty years, is but little more than the
legal interest of the nett money he has paid; the
rest is made up from those whose circumstances do
not require them to draw such support, and the
capital in both cases defrays the expences of government. It is on this ground that I have extended the probable claims to one third of the number of
aged persons in the nation.----Is it then better that
the lives of one hundred and forty thousand aged
persons be rendered comfortable, or that a million
a year of public money be expended on any one
individual, and him often of the most worthless
or insignificant character? Let reason and justice,
let honour and humanity, let even hypocrisy, sycophancy and Mr. Burke, let George, let Louis,
Leopold, Frederic, Catharine, Cornwallis, or
Tippoo Saib, answer the question *.

The

---

* Reckoning the taxes by families, five to a family, each family
pays on an average, 12*l.* 17*s.* 6*d. per ann.* to this sum are to be
added the poor-rates. Though all pay taxes in the articles they
consume, all do not pay poor-rates. About two millions are exempted, some as not being house-keepers, others as not being
able, and the poor themselves who receive the relief. The average, therefore, of poor-rates on the remaining number, is forty
shillings for every family of five persons, which makes the whole
average amount of taxes and rates, 14*l.* 17*s.* 6*d.* For six persons, 17*l.* 17*s.* For seven persons, 20*l.* 16*s.* 6*d.*

The average of taxes in America, under the new or representative system of government, including the interest of the debt
contracted in the war, and taking the population at four million of
souls, which it now amounts to, and it is daily encreasing, is five
shillings

The sum thus remitted to the poor will be,

To two hundred and fifty-two thousand
poor families, containing six hun-
dred and thirty thousand children,   2,520,000

To one hundred and forty thousand aged
persons,   -   -   1,120,000

                       £ 3,640,000

There will then remain three hundred and sixty thousand pounds out of the four millions, part of which may be applied as follows:

After all the above cases are provided for, there will still be a number of families who, though not properly of the class of poor, yet find it difficult to give education to their children; and such children, under such a case, would be in a worse condition than if their parents were actually poor. A nation under a well regulated goverment, should permit none to remain uninstructed. It is monarchical and aristocratical government only that requires ignorance for its support.

Suppose then four hundred thousand children to be in this condition, which is a greater number

shillings per head, men, women, and children. The difference, therefore, between the two governments, is as under,

	England.			America.		
	l.	s.	d.	l.	s.	d.
For a family of five persons	14	17	6	1	5	0
For a family of six persons	17	17	0	1	10	0
For a family of seven persons	20	16	6	1	15	0

                        than

than ought to be fuppofed, after the provifions already made, the method will be,

To allow for each of thofe children ten fhillings a year for the expence of fchooling, for fix years each, which will give them fix months fchooling each year, and half a crown a year for paper and fpelling books.

The expence of this will be annually* £250,000

There will then remain one hundred and ten thoufand pounds.

Notwithftanding the great modes of relief which the beft inftituted and beft principled government may devife, there will ftill be a number of fmaller cafes, which it is good policy as well as beneficence in a nation to confider.

Were twenty fhillings to be given to every wo-man immediately on the birth of a child, who fhould make the demand, and none will make it

---

* Public fchools do not anfwer the general purpofe of the poor. They are chiefly in corporation towns, from which the country towns and villages are excluded; or if admitted, the diftance occafions a great lofs of time. Education, to be ufeful to the poor, fhould be on the fpot; and the beft method, I be-lieve, to accomplifh this, is to enable the parents to pay the ex-pence themfelves. There are always perfons of both fexes to be found in every village, efpecially when growing into years, ca-pable of fuch an undertaking. Twenty children, at ten fhillings each, (and that not more than fix months each year) would be as much as fome livings amount to in the remote parts of England; and there are often diftreffed clergymen's widows to whom fuch an income would be acceptable. Whatever is given on this ac-count to children anfwers two purpofes, to them it is education, to thofe who educate them it is a livelihood.

beyond

whofe circumftances do not require it, it might relieve a great deal of inftant diftrefs.

There are about two hundred thoufand births
yearly in England ; and if claimed, by one fourth,

The amount would be   -   50,000

And twenty fhillings to every new-married
couple who fhould claim in like manner. This
would not exceed the fum of   -   £ 20,000

Alfo twenty thoufand pounds to be appropriated
to defray the funeral expences of perfons, who,
travelling for work, may die at a diftance from their
friends. By relieving parifhes from this charge,
the fick ftranger will be better treated.

I fhall finifh this part of the fubject with a plan
adapted to the particular condition of a metropolis, fuch as London.

Cafes are continually occurring in a metropolis
different to thofe which occur·in the country, and
for which a different, or rather an additional mode
of relief is neceffary. In the country, even in
large towns, people have a knowledge of each
other, and diftrefs never rifes to that extreme
height it fometimes does in a metropolis. There
is no fuch thing in the country as perfons, in the
literal fenfe of the word, ftarved to death, or dying
with cold from the want of a lodging. Yet fuch
cafes, and others equally as miferable, happen in
London.

Many a youth comes up to London full of expectations, and with little or no money, and unlefs he gets immediate employment he is already

half

half undone; and boys bred up in London without any means of a livelihood, and as it often happens of diffolute parents, are in a ftill worfe condition; and fervants long out of place are not much
better off. In fhort, a world of little cafes are
continually arifing, which bufy or affluent life knows
not of, to open the firft door to diftrefs. Hunger
is not among the poftponeable wants, and a day,
even a few hours, in fuch a condition, is often the
crifis of a life of ruin.

Thefe circumftances, which are the general caufe
of the little thefts and pilferings that lead to
greater, may be prevented. There yet remain
twenty thoufand pounds out of the four millions
of furplus taxes, which, with another fund hereafter to be mentioned, amounting to about twenty
thoufand pounds more, cannot be better applied
than to this purpofe. The plan then will be,

Firft, To erect two or more buildings, or take
fome already erected, capable of containing at leaft
fix thoufand perfons, and to have in each of thefe
places as many kinds of employment as can be
contrived, fo that every perfon who fhall come
may find fomething which he or fhe can do.

Secondly, To receive all who fhall come, without enquiring who or what they are. The only
condition to be, that for fo much, or fo many hours
work, each perfon fhall receive fo many meals of
wholefome food, and a warm lodging, at leaft as
good as a barrack. That a certain portion of what
each perfon's work fhall be worth fhall be referved,
and

and given to him, or her, on their going away ; and
that each perfon fhall ftay as long, or as fhort time,
or come as often as he chufe, on thefe conditions.

If each perfon ftaid three months, it would affift
by rotation twenty-four thoufand perfons annually,
though the real number, at all times, would be but
fix thoufand. By eftablifhing an afylum of this
kind, fuch perfons to whom temporary diftreffes
occur, would have an opportunity to recruit themfelves, and be enabled to look out for better employment.

Allowing that their labour paid but one half the
expence of fupporting them, after referving a portion of their earnings for themfelves, the fum of
forty thoufand pounds additional would defray all
other charges for even a greater number than fix
thoufand.

The fund very properly convertible to this purpofe, in addition to the twenty thoufand pounds, remaining of the former fund, will be the produce of
the tax upon coals, and fo iniquitoufly and wantonly
applied to the fupport of the Duke of Richmond.
It is horrid that any man, more efpecially at the
price coals now are, fhould live on the diftreffes of
a community ; and any government permitting
fuch an abufe, deferves to be difmiffed. This fund
is faid to be about twenty thoufand pounds *per
annum.*

I fhall

I shall now conclude this plan with enumerating the several particulars, and then proceed to other matters.

The enumeration is as follows :

First, Abolition of two million poor-rates.

Secondly, Provision for two hundred and fifty-two thousand poor families.

Thirdly, Education for one million and thirty thousand children.

Fourthly, Comfortable provision for one hundred and forty thousand aged persons.

Fifthly, Donation of twenty shillings each for fifty thousand births.

Sixthly, Donation of twenty shillings each for twenty thousand marriages.

1 Seventhly, Allowance of twenty thousand pounds for the funeral expences of persons travelling for work, and dying at a distance from their friends.

Eighthly, Employment, at all times, for the casual poor in the cities of London and Westminster.

By the operation of this plan, the poor laws, those instruments of civil torture, will be superceded, and the wasteful expence of litigation prevented. The hearts of the humane will not be shocked by ragged and hungry children, and persons of seventy and eighty years of age begging for bread. The dying poor will not be dragged from place to place to breathe their last, as a reprisal of parish upon parish. Widows will have a maintenance for their children, and not be carted away, on the death of their husbands, like culprits and criminals,

and

and children will no longer be confidered as encreafing the diftreffes of their parents. The haunts
of the wretched will be known, becaufe it will be to
their advantage, and the number of petty crimes,
the offspring of diftrefs and poverty, will be leffened.
The poor, as well as the rich, will then be interefted
in the fupport of government, and the caufe and
apprehenfion of riots and tumults will ceafe.—Ye
who fit in eafe, and folace yourfelves in plenty,
and fuch there are in Turkey and Ruffia, as well
as in England, and who fay to yourfelves, " Are
" we not well off," have ye thought of thefe
things ? When ye do, ye will ceafe to fpeak and
feel for yourfelves alone.

The plan is eafy in practice. It does not embarrafs trade by a fudden interruption in the order
of taxes, but effects the relief by changing the application of them ; and the money neceffary for the
purpofe can be drawn from the excife collections,
which are made eight times a year in every market
town in England.

Having now arranged and concluded this fubject, I proceed to the next.

Taking the prefent current expences at feven
millions and an half, which is the leaft amount
they are now at, there will remain (after the fum
of one million and an half be taken for the new current expences, and four millions for the before-
mentioned fervice) the fum of two millions; part
of which to be applied as follows :

Though

Though fleets and armies, by an alliance with France, will, in a great meafure, become ufelefs, yet the perfons who have devoted themfelves to thofe fervices, and have thereby unfitted themfelves for other lines of life, are not to be fufferers by the means that make others happy. They are a different defcription of men to thofe who form or hang about a court.

A part of the army will remain at leaft for fome years, and alfo of the navy, for which a provifion is already made in the former part of this plan of one million, which is almoft half a million more than the peace eftablifhment of the army and navy in the prodigal times of Charles the Second.

Suppofe then fifteen thoufand foldiers to be difbanded, and to allow to each of thofe men three fhillings a week during life, clear of all deductions, to be paid in the fame manner as the Chelfea College penfioners are paid, and for them to return to their trades and their friends; and alfo to add fifteen thoufand fixpences per week to the pay of the foldiers who fhall remain; the annual expence will be,

To the pay of fifteen thoufand
   difbanded foldiers, at three
   fhillings per week,   £ 117,000
Additional pay to the remaining foldiers,   -   19,500

      Carried forward -   136,500

                      Suppofe

Brought over	136,500
Suppose that the pay to the officers of the disbanded corps be of the same amount as the sum allowed to the men,	117,000
	253,500
To prevent bulky estimations, admit the same sum to the disbanded navy as to the army, and the same increase of pay, - - -	253,500
Total	507,000

Every year some part of this sum of half a million (I omit the odd seven thousand pounds for the purpose of keeping the account unembarrassed) will fall in, and the whole of it in time, as it is on the ground of life annuities, except the encreased pay of twenty-nine thousand pounds. As it falls in, a part of the taxes may be taken off; for instance, when thirty thousand pounds fall in the duty on hops may be wholly taken off; and as other parts fall in, the duties on candles and soap may be lessened, till at last they will totally cease.

There now remains at least one million and an half of surplus taxes.

The tax on houses and windows is one of those direct taxes, which, like the poor rates, is not confounded with trade; and, when taken off, the relief
lief

lief will be inftantly felt.   This tax falls heavy on the middling clafs of people.

The amount of this tax by the returns of 1788, was,

Houfes and windows by the act	*l.*	*s.*	*d.*
of 1766, —	385,459	11	7
Ditto ditto by the act			
of 1779, —	130,739	14	5½
Total	516,199	6	0½

If this tax be ftruck off, there will then remain about one million of furplus taxes, and as it is always proper to keep a fum in referve, for incidental matters, it may be beft not to extend reductions further, in the firft inftance, but to confider what may be accomplifhed by other modes of reform.

Among the taxes moft heavily felt is the commutation tax.   I fhall, therefore, offer a plan for its abolition, by fubftituting another in its place, which will affect three objects at once:

Firft, That of removing the burthen to where it can beft be borne.

Secondly, Reftoring juftice among families by a diftribution of property.

Thirdly, Extirpating the overgrown influence arifing from the unnatural law of primogeniture, and which is one of the principal fources of corruption at elections.

The

The amount of the commutation
   tax by the returns of 1788,
   was,   —————   £771,657 0 0

When taxes are propofed, the country is amufed by the plaufible language of taxing luxuries. One thing is called a luxury at one time, and fomething elfe at another; but the real luxury does not confift in the article, but in the means of procuring it, and this is always kept out of fight.

I know not why any plant or herb of the field fhould be a greater luxury in one country than another, but an overgrown eftate in either is a luxury at all times, and as fuch is the proper object of taxation. It is, therefore, right to take thofe kind tax-making gentlemen up on their own word, and argue on the principle themfelves have laid down, that of *taxing luxuries.* If they, or their champion Mr. Burke, who, I fear, is growing out of date like the man in armour, can prove that an eftate of twenty, thirty, or forty thoufand pounds a year is not a luxury, I will give up the argument.

Admitting that any annual fum, fay for inftance, one thoufand pounds, is neceffary or fufficient for the fupport of a family, confequently the fecond thoufand is of the nature of a luxury, the third ftill more fo, and by proceeding on, we fhall at laft arrive at a fum that may not improperly be called a prohibitable luxury. It would be impolitic to fet bounds to property acquired by induftry, and therefore it is right to place the prohibition

4   beyond

beyond the probable acquifition to which induſtry can extend; but there ought to be a limit to property, or the accumulation of it, by bequeſt. It ſhould paſs in ſome other line. The richeſt in every nation have poor relations, and thoſe often very near in conſanguinity.

The following table of progreſſive taxation is conſtructed on the above principles, and as a ſubſtitute for the commutation tax. It will reach the point of prohibition by a regular operation, and thereby ſupercede the ariſtocratical law of primogeniture.

T A B L E I.

A tax on all eſtates of the clear yearly value o fifty pounds, after deducting the land tax, and up

	s.	d.	
To £ 500 —	0	3	per pound
From 500 to 1000 —	0	6	per pound
On the ſecond thouſand	0	9	per pound
On the third ditto —	1	0	per pound
On the fourth ditto	1	6	per pound
On the fifth ditto —	2	0	per pound
On the ſixth ditto —	3	0	per pound
On the ſeventh ditto	4	0	per pound
On the eighth ditto	5	0	per pound
On the ninth ditto —	6	0	per pound
On the tenth ditto —	7	0	per pound
On the eleventh ditto	8	0	per pound
On the twelfth ditto	9	0	per pound

On

	s.	d.	
On the thirteenth ditto	10	0	per pound
On the fourteenth ditto	11	0	per pound
On the fifteenth ditto	12	0	per pound
On the sixteenth ditto	13	0	per pound
On the seventeenth ditto	14	0	per pound
On the eighteenth ditto	15	0	per pound
On the nineteenth ditto	16	0	per pound
On the twentieth ditto	17	0	per pound
On the twenty-first ditto	18	0	per pound
On the twenty-second ditto	19	0	per pound
On the twenty-third ditto	20	0	per pound

The foregoing table shews the progression per pound on every progressive thousand. The following table shews the amount of the tax on every thousand separately, and in the last column, the total amount of all the separate sums collected.

TABLE II.

	d.	l.	s.	d.
An estate of £ 50 *per ann.* at 3 per pd. pays		0	12	6
100	3	1	5	0
200	3	2	10	0
300	3	3	15	0
400	3	5	0	0
500	3	7	5	0

After

After 500*l.*—the tax of fixpence per pound takes place on the fecond 500*l.*—confequently an eftate of 1000*l. per ann.* pays 21*l.* 15*s.* and fo on,

		l.	*s.*	*d.*		*l.*	*s.*	Total amount. *l.*	*s.*
1ft	500 at	0	3	per pound	7	5 ⎫		21	15
2d	500 at	0	6		14	10 ⎭			
2d	1000 at	0	9		37	10	59	5
3d	1000 at	1	0		50	0	109	5
4th	1000 at	1	6		75	0	184	5
5th	1000 at	2	0		100	0	284	5
6th	1000 at	3	0		150	0	434	5
7th	1000 at	4	0		200	0	634	5
8th	1000 at	5	0		250	0	880	5
9th	1000 at	6	0		300	0	1180	5
10th	1000 at	7	0		350	0	1530	5
11th	1000 at	8	0		400	0	1930	5
12th	1000 at	9	0		450	0	2380	5
13th	1000 at	10	0		500	0	2880	5
14th	1000 at	11	0		550	0	3430	5
15th	1000 at	12	0		600	0	4030	5
16th	1000 at	13	0		650	0	4680	5
17th	1000 at	14	0		700	0	5380	5
18th	1000 at	15	0		750	0	6130	5
19th	1000 at	16	0		800	0	6930	5
20th	1000 at	17	0		850	0	7780	5
21ft	1000 at	18	0		900	0	8680	5
22d	1000 at	19	0		950	0	9630	5
23d	1000 at	20	0		1000	0	10630	5

At

At the twenty-third thousand the tax becomes twenty shillings in the pound, and consequently every thousand beyond that sum can produce no profit but by dividing the estate. Yet formidable as this tax appears, it will not, I believe, produce so much as the commutation tax; should it produce more, it ought to be lowered to that amount upon estates under two or three thousand a year.

On small and middling estates it is lighter (as it is intended to be) than the commutation tax. It is not till after seven or eight thousand a year that it begins to be heavy. The object is not so much the produce of the tax, as the justice of the measure. The aristocracy has screened itself too much, and this serves to restore a part of the lost equilibrium.

As an instance of its screening itself, it is only necessary to look back to the first establishment of the excise laws, at what is called the Restoration, or the coming of Charles the Second. The aristocratical interest then in power, commuted the feudal services itself was under by laying a tax on beer brewed for *sale*; that is, they compounded with Charles for an exemption from those services for themselves and their heirs, by a tax to be paid by other people. The aristocracy do not purchase beer brewed for sale, but brew their own beer free of the duty, and if any commutation at that time were necessary, it ought to have been at the expence of those for whom the exemptions from those ser-

L   vices

vices were intended *; inftead of which it was thrown on an entire different clafs of men.

But the chief object of this progreffive tax (befides the juftice of rendering taxes more equal than they are) is, as already ftated, to extirpate the overgrown influence arifing from the unnatural law of primogeniture, and which is one of the principal fources of corruption at elections.

It would be attended with no good confequences to enquire how fuch vaft eftates as thirty, forty, or fifty thoufand a year could commence, and that at a time when commerce and manufactures were not in a ftate to admit of fuch acquifitions. Let it be fufficient to remedy the evil by putting them in a condition of defcending again to the community, by the quiet means of apportioning them among all the heirs and heireffes of thofe families. This will be the more neceffary, becaufe hitherto the ariftocracy have quartered their younger children and connections upon the public in ufelefs pofts, places, and offices, which when abolifhed will leave them deftitute, unlefs the law of primogeniture be alfo abolifhed or fuperceded.

A progreffive tax will, in a great meafure, effect this object, and that as a matter of intereft to the

* The tax on beer brewed for fale, from which the ariftocracy are exempt, is almoft one million more than the prefent commutation tax, being by the returns of 1788, 1,666,152l. and confequently they ought to take on themfelves the amount of the commutation tax, as they are already exempted from one which is almoft one million greater.

parties moft immediately concerned, as will be feen by the following table; which fhews the nett produce upon every eftate, after fubtracting the tax. By this it will appear, that after an eftate exceeds thirteen or fourteen thoufand a year, the remainder produces but little profit to the holder, and confequently will pafs either to the younger children, or to other kindred.

TABLE III.

Shewing the nett produce of every eftate from one thoufand to twenty-three thoufand pounds a year.

No. of thoufands per ann.	Total tax fubtracted. £.	Nett produce. £.
1000	21	979
2000	59	1941
3000	109	2891
4000	184	3816
5000	284	4716
6000	434	5566
7000	634	6366
8000	880	7120
9000	1180	7820
10,000	1530	8470
11,000	1930	9070
12,000	2380	9620
13,000	2880	10,120
14,000	3430	10,570
15,000	4030	10,970
16,000		

	£.	£.
16,000	4680	11,320
17,000	5380	11,620
18,000	6130	11,870
19,000	6930	12,170
20,000	7780	12,220
21,000	8680	12,320
22,000	9630	12,370
23,000	10,630	12,370

N. B. The odd shillings are dropped in this table.

According to this table, an estate cannot produce more then 12,370*l.* clear of the land tax and the progressive tax, and therefore the dividing such estates will follow as a matter of family interest. An estate of 23,000*l.* a year, divided into five estates of four thousand each and one of three, will be charged only 1129*l.* which is but five *per cent.* but if held by one possessor will be charged 10,630*l.*

Although an enquiry into the origin of those estates be unnecessary, the continuation of them in their present state is another subject. It is a matter of national concern. As hereditary estates, the law has created the evil, and it ought also to provide the remedy. Primogeniture ought to be abolished, not only because it is unnatural and unjust, but because the country suffers by its operation. By cutting off (as before observed) the younger children from their proper portion of inheritance, the public is

loaded

loaded with the expence of maintaining them; and the freedom of elections violated by the overbearing influence which this unjust monopoly of family property produces. Nor is this all. It occasions a waste of national property. A considerable part of the land of the country is rendered unproductive by the great extent of parks and chases which this law serves to keep up, and this at a time when the annual production of grain is not equal to the national consumption *.—In short, the evils of the aristocratical system are so great and numerous, so inconsistent with every thing that is just, wise, natural, and beneficent, that when they are considered, there ought not to be a doubt that many, who are now classed under that description, will wish to see such a system abolished.

What pleasure can they derive from contemplating the exposed condition, and almost certain beggary of their younger offspring? Every aristocratical family has an appendage of family beggars hanging round it, which in a few ages, or a few generations, are shook off, and console themselves with telling their tale in alms-houses, work-houses, and prisons. This is the natural consequence of aristocracy. The peer and the beggar are often of the same family. One extreme produces the other: to make one rich many must be made poor; neither can the system be supported by other means.

* See the reports on the corn trade

There

There are two claffes of people to whom the laws of England are particularly hoftile, and thofe the moft helplefs; younger children and the poor. Of the former I have juft fpoken; of the latter I fhall mention one inftance out of the many that might be produced, and with which I fhall clofe this fubject.

Several laws are in exiftence for regulating and limiting workmen's wages. Why not leave them as free to make their own bargains, as the law-makers are to let their farms and houfes? Perfonal labour is all the property they have. Why is that little, and the little freedom they enjoy to be infringed? But the injuftice will appear ftronger, if we confider the operation and effect of fuch laws. When wages are fixed by what is called a law, the legal wages remain ftationary, while every thing elfe is in progreffion; and as thofe who make that law, ftill continue to lay on new taxes by other laws, they encreafe the expence of living by one law, and take away the means by another.

But if thofe gentlemen law-makers and tax-makers thought it right to limit the poor pittance which perfonal labour can produce, and on which a whole family is to be fupported, they certainly muft feel themfelves happily indulged in a limitation on their own part, of not lefs than twelve thoufand a year, and that of property they never acquired, (nor probably any of their anceftors) and of which they have made fo ill a ufe.

Having

Having now finifhed this fubject, I fhall bring the feveral particulars into one view, and then proceed to other matters.

The firft EIGHT ARTICLES are brought forward from page 136.

1. Abolition of two million poor-rates.

2. Provifion for two hundred and fifty-two thoufand poor families, at the rate of four pounds per head for each child under fourteen years of age; which, with the addition of two hundred and fifty thoufand pounds, provides alfo education for one million and thirty thoufand children.

3. Annuity of fix pounds (per ann.) each for all poor perfons, decayed tradefmen, or others (fuppofed feventy thoufand) of the age of fifty years, and until fixty.

4. Annuity of ten pounds each for life for all poor perfons, decayed tradefmen, and others (fuppofed feventy thoufand) of the age of fixty years.

5. Donation of twenty fhillings each for fifty thoufand births.

6. Donation of twenty fhillings each for twenty thoufand marriages.

7. Allowance of twenty thoufand pounds for the funeral expences of perfons travelling for work, and dying at a diftance from their friends.

8. Employment at all times for the cafual poor in the cities of London and Weftminfter.

9. Aboli-

SECOND ENUMERATION.

9. Abolition of the tax on houfes and windows.

10. Allowance of three fhillings per week for life to fifteen thoufand difbanded foldiers, and a proportionable allowance to the officers of the difbanded corps.

11. Encreafe of pay to the remaining foldiers of 19,500*l.* annually.

12. The fame allowance to the difbanded navy, and the fame encreafe of pay, as to the army.

13. Abolition of the commutation tax.

14. Plan of a progreffive tax, operating to extirpate the unjuft and unnatural law of primogeniture, and the vicious influence of the ariftocratical fyftem *.

There yet remains, as already ftated, one million of furplus taxes. Some part of this will be required for circumftances that do not immediately prefent themfelves, and fuch part as fhall not be wanted, will admit a further reduction of taxes equal to that amount.

Among

---

* When enquiries are made into the condition of the poor, various degrees of diftrefs will moft probably be found, to render a different arrangement preferable to that which is already propofed. Widows with families will be in greater want than where there are hufbands living. There is alfo a difference in the expence of living in different countries; and more fo in fuel.

Among the claims that juftice requires to be made, the condition of the inferior revenue officers will merit attention. It is a reproach to any government to wafte fuch an immenfity of revenue in finecures and nominal and unneceffary places and offices, and not allow even a decent livelihood to thofe on whom the labour falls. The falary of the inferior officers of the revenue has ftood at the petty pittance of lefs than fifty pounds a year for upwards of one hundred years. It ought to be feventy. About one hundred and twenty thoufand pounds applied to this purpofe, will put all thofe falaries in a decent condition.

This was propofed to be done almoft twenty years ago, but the treafury-board then in being

	£.
Suppofe then fifty thoufand extraordinary cafes, at the rate of 10l. per family per ann. ———	500,000
100,000 Families, at 8l. per family per ann. -	800,000
100,000 Families, at 7l. per family per ann. -	700,000
104,000 Families, at 5l. per family per ann.	520,000
And inftead of ten fhillings per head for the education of other children, to allow fifty fhillings per family for that purpofe to fifty thoufand families	250,000
	2,770,000
140,000 Aged perfons as before.	1,120,000
	3,890,000

This arrangement amounts to the fame fum as ftated in page 131, including the 250,000l. for education; but it provides (including the aged people) for four hundred and four thoufand families, which is almoft one third of all the families in England.

ftartled

startled at it, as it might lead to similar expectations from the army and navy ; and the event was,
that the King, or somebody for him, applied to
parliament to have his own salary raised an hundred thousand a year, which being done, every
thing else was laid aside.

With respect to another class of men, the inferior clergy, I forbear to enlarge on their condition; but all partialities and prejudices for, or
against, different modes and forms of religion aside,
common justice will determine, whether there
ought to be an income of twenty or thirty pounds
a year to one man, and of ten thousand to another.
I speak on this subject with the more freedom,
because I am known not to be a Presbyterian;
and therefore the cant cry of court sycophants,
about church and meeting, kept up to amuse and
bewilder the nation, cannot be raised against me.

Ye simple men, on both sides the question, do
ye not see through this courtly craft ? If ye can be
kept disputing and wiangling about church and
meeting, ye just answer the purpose of every courtier, who lives the while on the spoil of the taxes, and
laughs at your credulity. Every religion is good that
teaches man to be good ; and I know of none that
instructs him to be bad.

All the before-mentioned calculations, suppose
only sixteen millions and an half of taxes paid into
the exchequer, after the expence of collection and
drawbacks at the custom-house and excise-office

are

are deducted; whereas the fum paid into the exchequer is very nearly, if not quite, feventeen millions. The taxes raifed in Scotland and Ireland are expended in thofe countries, and therefore their favings will come out of their own taxes; but if any part be paid into the Englifh exchequer, it might be remitted. This will not make one hundred thoufand pounds a year difference.

There now remains only the national debt to be confidered. In the year 1789, the intereft, exclufive of the tontine, was 9,150,138*l.* How much the capital has been reduced fince that time the minifter beft knows. But after paying the intereft, abolifhing the tax on houfes and windows, the commutation tax, and the poor rates; and making all the provifions for the poor, for the education of children, the fupport of the aged, the difbanded part of the army and navy, and encreafing the pay of the remainder, there will be a furplus of one million.

The prefent fcheme of paying off the national debt appears to me, fpeaking as an indifferent perfon, to be an ill-concerted, if not a fallacious job. The burthen of the national debt confifts not in its being fo many millions, or fo many hundred millions, but in the quantity of taxes collected every year to pay the intereft. If this quantity continue the fame, the burthen of the national debt is the fame to all intents and purpofes, be the capital more or lefs. The only knowledge which

which the public can have of the reduction of the
debt, muſt be through the reduction of taxes for
paying the intereſt. The debt, therefore, is not
reduced one farthing to the public by all the millions that have been paid; and it would require
more money now to purchaſe up the capital, than
when the ſcheme began.

Digreſſing for a moment at this point, to which
I ſhall return again, I look back to the appoint-
ment of Mr. Pitt, as miniſter.

I was then in America. The war was over;
and though reſentment had ceaſed, memory was
ſtill alive.

When the news of the coalition arrived, though
it was a matter of no concern to me as a citizen of
America, I felt it as a man. It had ſomething
in it which ſhocked, by publicly ſporting with de-
cency, if not with principle. It was impudence in
Lord North; it was want of firmneſs in Mr. Fox.

Mr. Pitt was, at that time, what may be called
a maiden character in politics. So far from being
hackneyed, he appeared not to be initiated into
the firſt myſteries of court intrigue. Every thing
was in his favour. Reſentment againſt the coalition ſerved as friendſhip to him, and his ignorance
of vice was credited for virtue. With the return of
peace, commerce and proſperity would riſe of itſelf;
yet even this encreaſe was thrown to his account.

When he came to the helm the ſtorm was over,
and he had nothing to interrupt his courſe. It required

quired even ingenuity to be wrong, and he suc-
ceeded. A little time shewed him the same sort
of man as his predecessors had been. Instead of
profiting by those errors which had accumulated a
burthen of taxes unparalleled in the world, he
sought, I might almost say, he advertised for enemies, and provoked means to encrease taxation.
Aiming at something, he knew not what, he ran-
facked Europe and India for adventures, and aban-
doning the fair pretensions he began with, became
the knight-errant of modern times.

It is unpleasant to see character throw itself
away. It is more so to see one's-self deceived.
Mr. Pitt had merited nothing, but he promised
much. He gave symptoms of a mind superior to
the meanness and corruption of courts. His apparent candour encouraged expectations; and
the public confidence, stunned, wearied, and
confounded by a chaos of parties, revived and
attached itself to him. But mistaking, as he has
done, the disgust of the nation against the coalition,
for merit in himself, he has rushed into measures,
which a man less supported would not have pre-
fumed to act.

All this seems to shew that change of ministers
amounts to nothing. One goes out, another comes
in, and still the same measures, vices, and extravagance are pursued. It signifies not who is minister. The defect lies in the system. The foun-
dation and the superstructure of the government
is

is bad. Prop it as you pleafe, it continually finks into court government, and ever will.

I return, as I promifed, to the fubject of the national debt, that offspring of the Dutch-Anglo revolution, and its handmaid the Hanover fuc-ceffion.

But it is now too late to enquire how it began. Thofe to whom it is due have advanced the mo-ney; and whether it was well or ill fpent, or pocketed, is not their crime. It is, however, eafy to fee, that as the nation proceeds in contemplat-ing the nature and principles of government, and to underftand taxes, and make comparifons be-tween thofe of America, France, and England, it will be next to impoffible to keep it in the fame torpid ftate it has hitherto been. Some re-form muft, from the neceffity of the cafe, foon begin. It is not whether thefe principles prefs with little or much force in the prefent moment. They are out. They are abroad in the world, and no force can ftop them. Like a fecret told, they are beyond recall; and he muft be blind indeed that does not fee that a change is already beginning.

Nine millions of dead taxes is a ferious thing; and this not only for bad, but in a great meafure for foreign government. By putting the power of making war into the hands of foreigners who came for what they could get, little elfe was to be ex-pected than what has happened.

Reafons

Reaſons are already advanced in this work ſhewing that whatever the reforms in the taxes may be, they ought to be made in the current expences of government, and not in the part applied to the intereſt of the national debt. By remitting the taxes of the poor, *they* will be totally relieved, and all diſcontent on their part will be taken away; and by ſtriking off ſuch of the taxes as are already mentioned, the nation will more than recover the whole expence of the mad American war.

There will then remain only the national debt as a ſubjeſt of diſcontent; and in order to remove, or rather to prevent this, it would be good policy in the ſtock-holders themſelves to conſider it as property, ſubjeſt like all other property, to bear ſome portion of the taxes. It would give to it both popularity and ſecurity, and as a great part of its preſent inconvenience is balanced by the capital which it keeps alive, a meaſure of this kind would ſo far add to that balance as to ſilence objeſtions.

This may be done by ſuch gradual means as to accompliſh all that is neceſſary with the greateſt eaſe and convenience.

Inſtead of taxing the capital, the beſt method would be to tax the intereſt by ſome progreſſive ratio, and to leſſen the public taxes in the ſame proportion as the intereſt diminiſhed.

Suppoſe the intereſt was taxed one halfpenny in the pound the firſt year, a penny more the ſecond,

and

and to proceed by a certain ratio to be determined upon, always lefs than any other tax upon property. Such a tax would be fubtracted from the intereft at the time of payment, without any expence of collection.

One halfpenny in the pound would leffen the intereft and confequently the taxes, twenty thoufand pounds. The tax on waggons amounts to this fum, and this tax might be taken off the firft year. The fecond year the tax on female fervants, or fome other of the like amount might alfo be taken off, and by proceeding in this manner, always applying the tax raifed from the property of the debt towards its extinction, and not carry it to the current fervices, it would liberate itfelf.

The ftockholders, notwithftanding this tax, would pay lefs taxes than they do now. What they would fave by the extinction of the poor-rates, and the tax on houfes and windows, and the commutation tax, would be confiderably greater than what this tax, flow, but certain in its operation, amounts to.

It appears to me to be prudence to look out for meafures that may apply under any circumftance that may approach. There is, at this moment, a crifis in the affairs of Europe that requires it. Preparation now is wifdom. If taxation be once let loofe, it will be difficult to re-inftate it; neither would the relief be fo effectual, as to proceed by fome certain and gradual reduction.

The

The fraud, hypocrify, and impofition of governments, are now beginning to be too well underftood to promife them any long career. The farce
of monarchy and ariftocracy, in all countries, is
following that of chivalry, and Mr. Burke is dref-
fing for the funeral. Let it then pafs quietly to
the tomb of all other follies, and the mourners be
comforted.

The time is not very diftant when England will
laugh at itfelf for fending to Holland, Hanover,
Zell, or Brunfwick for men, at the expence of a
million a year, who underftood neither her laws,
her language, nor her intereft, and whofe capaci-
ties would fcarcely have fitted them for the office
of a parifh conftable. If government could be
trufted to fuch hands, it muft be fome eafy and
fimple thing indeed, and materials fit for all the
purpofes may be found in every town and village
in England.

When it fhall be faid in any country in the
world, my poor are happy; neither ignorance nor
diftrefs is to be found among them; my jails are
empty of prifoners, my ftreets of beggars; the
aged are not in want, the taxes are not oppreffive;
the rational world is my friend, becaufe I am the
friend of its happinefs: when thefe things can be
faid, then may that country boaft its conftitution
and its government.

Within the fpace of a few years we have feen
two Revolutions, thofe of America and France. In
the former, the conteft was long, and the conflict fe-

M   vere;

vere; in the latter, the nation acted with such a
confolidated impulfe, that having no foreign enemy to contend with, the revolution was complete
in power the moment it appeared. From both
thofe inftances it is evident, that the greateft forces
that can be brought into the field of revolutions,
are reafon and common intereft. Where thefe can
have the opportunity of acting, oppofition dies
with fear, or crumbles away by conviction. It
is a great ftanding which they have now univerfally obtained; and we may hereafter hope to
fee revolutions, or changes in governments, produced with the fame quiet operation by which any
meafure, determinable by reafon and difcuffion, is
accomplifhed.

When a nation changes its opinion and habits of
thinking, it is no longer to be governed as before;
but it would not only be wrong, but bad policy,
to attempt by force what ought to be accomplifhed
by reafon. Rebellion confifts in forcibly oppofing the general will of a nation, whether by
a party or by a government. There ought, therefore, to be in every nation a method of occafionally
afcertaining the ftate of public opinion with refpect
to government. On this point the old government of France was fuperior to the prefent government of England, becaufe, on extraordinary
occafions, recourfe could be had to what was then
called the States General. But in England there
are no fuch occafional bodies; and as to thofe who
are now called Reprefentatives, a great part of
them

them are mere machines of the court, placemen, and dependants.

I prefume, that though all the people of England pay taxes, not an hundredth part of them are electors, and the members of one of the houfes of parliament reprefent nobody but themfelves. There is, therefore, no power but the voluntary will of the people that has a right to act in any matter refpecting a general reform; and by the fame right that two perfons can confer on fuch a fubject, a thoufand may. The object, in all fuch preliminary proceedings, is to find out what the general fenfe of a nation is, and to be governed by it. If it prefer a bad or defective government to a reform, or chufe to pay ten times more taxes than there is occafion for, it has a right fo to do; and fo long as the majority do not impofe conditions on the minority, different to what they impofe on themfelves, though there may be much error, there is no injuftice. Neither will the error continue long. Reafon and difcuffion will foon bring things right, however wrong they may begin. By fuch a procefs no tumult is to be apprehended. The poor, in all countries, are naturally both peaceable and grateful in all reforms in which their intereft and happinefs is included. It is only by neglecting and rejecting them that they become tumultuous.

The objects that now prefs on the public attention are, the French revolution, and the profpect of a general revolution in governments. Of all

nations

nations in Europe, there is none fo much interefted in the French revolution as England. Enemies for ages, and that at a vaft expence, and without any national object, the opportunity now prefents itfelf of amicably clofing the fcene, and joining their efforts to reform the reft of Europe. By doing this, they will not only prevent the further effufion of blood, and encreafe of taxes, but be in a condition of getting rid of a confiderable part of their prefent burthens, as has been already ftated. Long experience however has fhewn, that reforms of this kind are not thofe which old governments wifh to promote; and therefore it is to nations, and not to fuch governments, that thefe matters prefent themfelves.

In the preceding part of this work, I have fpoken of an alliance between England, France, and America, for purpofes that were to be afterwards mentioned. Though I have no direct authority on the part of America, I have good reafon to conclude, that fhe is difpofed to enter into a confideration of fuch a meafure, provided, that the governments with which fhe might ally, acted as national governments, and not as courts enveloped in intrigue and myftery. That France as a nation, and a national government, would prefer an alliance with England, is a matter of certainty. Nations, like individuals, who have long been enemies, without knowing each other, or knowing why, become the better friends when they difcover

the

the errors and impofitions under which they had acted.

Admitting, therefore, the probability of fuch a connection, I will ftate fome matters by which fuch an alliance, together with that of Holland, might render fervice, not only to the parties immediately concerned, but to all Europe.

It is, I think, certain, that if the fleets of England, France, and Holland were confederated, they could propofe, with effect, a limitation to, and a general difmantling of all the navies in Europe, to a certain proportion to be agreed upon.

Firft, That no new fhip of war fhall be built by any power in Europe, themfelves included.

Secondly, That all the navies now in exiftence fhall be put back, fuppofe to one-tenth of their prefent force. This will fave to France and England at leaft two millions fterling annually to each, and their relative force be in the fame proportion as it is now. If men will permit themfelves to think, as rational beings ought to think, nothing can appear more ridiculous and abfurd, exclufive of all moral reflections, than to be at the expence of building navies, filling them with men, and then hauling them into the ocean, to try which can fink each other fafteft. Peace, which cofts nothing, is attended with infinitely more advantage, than any victory with all its expence. But this, though it beft anfwers the purpofe of nations, does not that of court governments, whofe habited policy is pretence for taxation, places, and offices.

It

It is, I think, also certain, that the above confederated powers, together with that of the United States of America, can propose with effect, to Spain, the independance of South America, and the opening thofe countries of immenfe extent and wealth to the general commerce of the world, as North America now is.

With how much more glory, and advantage to itfelf, does a nation act, when it exerts its powers to refcue the world from bondage, and to create itfelf friends, than when it employs thofe powers to encreafe ruin, defolation, and mifery. The horrid fcene that is now acting by the Englifh government in the Eaft-Indies, is fit only to be told of Goths and Vandals, who, deftitute of principle, robbed and tortured the world they were incapable of enjoying.

The opening of South America would produce an immenfe field of commerce, and a ready money market for manufactures, which the eaftern world does not. The Eaft is already a country full of manufactures, the importation of which is not only an injury to the manufactures of England, but a drain upon its fpecie. The balance againft England by this trade is regularly upwards of half a million annually fent out in the Eaft-India fhips in filver; and this is the reafon, together with German intrigue, and German fubfidies, there is fo little filver in England.

But any war is harveft to fuch governments, however ruinous it may be to a nation. It ferves to

keep

keep up deceitful expectations which prevent a people looking into the defects and abuses of government. It is the *lo here!* and the *lo there!* that amuses and cheats the multitude.

Never did so great an opportunity offer itself to England, and to all Europe, as is produced by the two Revolutions of America and France. By the former, freedom has a national champion in the Western world; and by the latter, in Europe. When another nation shall join France, despotism and bad government will scarcely dare to appear. To use a trite expression, the iron is becoming hot all over Europe. The insulted German and the enslaved Spaniard, the Russ and the Pole, are beginning to think. The present age will hereafter merit to be called the Age of reason, and the present generation will appear to the future as the Adam of a new world.

When all the governments of Europe shall be established on the representative system, nations will become acquainted, and the animosities and prejudices fomented by the intrigue and artifice of courts, will cease. The oppressed soldier will become a freeman; and the tortured sailor, no longer dragged along the streets like a felon, will pursue his mercantile voyage in safety. It would be better that nations should continue the pay of their soldiers during their lives, and give them their discharge and restore them to freedom and their friends, and cease recruiting, than retain such multitudes at the same expence, in a condition useless

M 4

to fociety and themfelves. As foldiers have hitherto been treated in moft countries, they might be
faid to be without a friend. Shunned by the citizen on an apprehenfion of being enemies to liberty, and too often infulted by thofe who commanded them, their condition was a double oppreffion. But where genuine principles of liberty
pervade a people, every thing is reftored to order;
and the foldier civily treated, returns the civi-
lity.

In contemplating revolutions, it is eafy to perceive that they may arife from two diftinct caufes;
the one, to avoid or get rid of fome great calamity;
the other, to obtain fome great and pofitive good;
and the two may be diftinguifhed by the names of
active and paffive revolutions. In thofe which
proceed from the former caufe, the temper becomes incenfed and fowered; and the redrefs, obtained by danger, is too often fullied by revenge.
But in thofe which proceed from the latter, the
heart, rather animated than agitated, enters fe-
renely upon the fubject. Reafon and difcuffion,
perfuafion and conviction, become the weapons in
the conteft, and it is only when thofe are attempted
to be fuppreffed that recource is had to violence.
When men unite in agreeing that a *thing is good*,
could it be obtained, fuch as relief from a burden
of taxes and the extinction of corruption, the object is more than half accomplifhed. What they
approve as the end, they will promote in the
means.

Will

Will any man fay, in the prefent excefs of taxation, falling fo heavily on the poor, that a remif-
fion of five pounds annually of taxes to one hundred and four thoufand poor families is not a *good
thing?* Will he fay, that a remiffion of feven
pounds annually to one hundred thoufand other
poor families—of eight pounds annually to another
hundred thoufand poor families, and of ten pounds
annually to fifty thoufand poor and widowed families, are not *good things?* And to proceed a ftep
farther in this climax, will he fay, that to provide
againft the misfortunes to which all human life is
fubject, by fecuring fix pounds annually for all poor,
diftreffed, and reduced perfons of the age of fifty
and until fixty, and of ten pounds annually after
fixty is not a *good thing?*

Will he fay, that an abolition of two million of
poor-rates to the houfe-keepers, and of the whole
of the houfe and window-light tax and of the commutation tax is not a *good thing?* Or will he fay,
that to abolifh corruption is a *bad thing?*

If, therefore, the good to be obtained be worthy
of a paffive, rational, and coftlefs revolution, it
would be bad policy to prefer waiting for a calamity that fhould force a violent one. I have no
idea, confidering the reforms which are now paffing
and fpreading throughout Europe, that England
will permit herfelf to be the laft; and where the
occafion and the opportunity quietly offer, it is
better than to wait for a turbulent neceffity. It
may be confidered as an honour to the animal facul-

ties of man to obtain redrefs by courage and danger, but it is far greater honour to the rational faculties to accomplifh the fame object by reafon, accommodation, and general confent *.

As reforms, or revolutions, call them which you pleafe, extend themfelves among nations, thofe nations will form connections and conventions, and when a few are thus confederated, the progrefs will be rapid, till defpotifm and corrupt government be totally expelled, at leaft out of two quarters of the world, Europe and America. The Algerine piracy may then be commanded to ceafe, for it is only by the malicious policy of old governments, againft each other, that it exifts.

* I know it is the opinion of many of the moft enlightened characters in France (there always will be thofe who fee farther into events than others) not only among the general mafs of citizens, but of many of the principal members of the former National Affembly, that the monarchical plan will not continue many years in that country. They have found out, that as wifdom cannot be made hereditary, power ought not; and that, for a man to merit a million ftirling a year from a nation, he ought to have a mind capable of comprehending from an atom to a univerfe; which, if he had, he would be above receiving the pay. But they wifhed not to appear to lead the nation fafter than its own reafon and intereft dictated. In all the converfations where I have been prefent upon this fubject, the idea always was, that when fuch a time, from the general opinion of the nation, fhall arrive, that the honourable and liberal method would be, to make a handfome prefent in fee fimple to the perfon whoever he may be, that fhall then be in the monarchical office, and for him to retire to the enjoyment of private life, poffeffing his fhare of general rights and privileges, and to be no more accountable to the public for his time and his conduct than any other citizen.

Throughout

Throughout this work, various and numerous as the fubjects are, which I have taken up and inveftigated, there is only a fingle paragraph upon religion, viz. " *that every religion is good, that* " *teaches man to be good.*"

I have carefully avoided to enlarge upon the fubject, becaufe I am inclined to believe, that what is called the prefent miniftry wifh to fee contentions about religion kept up, to prevent the nation turning its attention to fubjects of government. It is, as if they were to fay, " *Look that* " *way, or any way, but this.*"

But as religion is very improperly made a political machine, and the reality of it is thereby deftroyed, I will conclude this work with ftating in what light religion appears to me.

If we fuppofe a large family of children, who, on any particular day, or particular circumftance, made it a cuftom to prefent to their parent fome token of their affection and gratitude, each of them would make a different offering, and moft probably in a different manner. Some would pay their congratulations in themes of verfe or profe, by fome little devices, as their genius dictated, or according to what they thought would pleafe ; and, perhaps, the leaft of all, not able to do any of thofe things, would ramble into the garden, or the field, and gather what it thought the prettieft flower it could find, though, perhaps, it might be but a fimple weed. The parent would be more gratified by fuch variety, than if the whole of
                                        them

them had acted on a concerted plan, and each had made exactly the same offering. This would have the cold appearance of contrivance, or the harſh one of controul. But of all unwelcome things, nothing could more afflict the parent than to know, that the whole of them had afterwards gotten together by the ears, boys and girls, fighting, ſcratching, reviling, and abuſing each other about which was the beſt or the worſt preſent.

Why may we not ſuppoſe, that the great Father of all is pleaſed with variety of devotion ; and that the greateſt offence we can act, is that by which we ſeek to torment and render each other miſerable. For my own part, I am fully ſatisfied that what I am now doing, with an endeavour to conciliate mankind, to render their condition happy, to unite nations that have hitherto been enemies, and to extirpate the horrid practice of war, and break the chains of ſlavery and oppreſſion, is acceptable in his ſight, and being the beſt ſervice I can perform, I act it chearfully.

I do not believe that any two men, on what are called doctrinal points, think alike who think at all. It is only thoſe who have not thought that appear to agree. It is in this caſe as with what is called the Britiſh conſtitution. It has been taken for granted to be good, and encomiums have ſupplied the place of proof. But when the nation come to examine into its principles and the abuſes it admits, it will be found to have more defects than I have pointed out in this work and the former.

As to what are called national religions, we

may,

may, with as much propriety, talk of national Gods. It is either political craft or the remains of the Pagan fyftem, when every nation had its feparate and particular deity. Among all the writers of the Englifh church clergy, who have treated on the general fubject of religion, the prefent Bifhop of Landaff has not been excelled, and it is with much pleafure that I take the opportunity of expreffing this token of refpect.

I have now gone through the whole of the fubject, at leaft, as far as it appears to me at prefent. It has been my intention for the five years I have been in Europe, to offer an addrefs to the people of England on the fubject of government, if the opportunity prefented itfelf before I returned to America. Mr. Burke has thrown it in my way, and I thank him. On a certain occafion three years ago, I preffed him to propofe a national convention to be fairly elected for the purpofe of taking the ftate of the nation into confideration; but I found, that however ftrongly the parliamentary current was then fetting againft the party he acted with, their policy was to keep every thing within that field of corruption, and truft to accidents. Long experience had fhewn that parliaments would follow any change of minifters, and on this they refted their hopes and their expectations.

Formerly, when divifions arofe refpecting governments, recourfe was had to the fword, and a civil war enfued. That favage cuftom is exploded by the new fyftem, and reference is had to national conventions. Difcuffion and the general will arbitrates

bitrates the queſtion, and to this, private opinion yields with a good grace, and order is preſerved uninterrupted.

Some gentlemen have affeſted to call the principles upon which this work and the former part of *Rights of Man* are founded, " a new fangled doctrine." The queſtion is not whether thoſe principles are new or old, but whether they are right or wrong. Suppoſe the former, I will ſhew their effeſt by a figure eaſily underſtood.

It is now towards the middle of February. Were I to take a turn into the country, the trees would preſent a leafleſs winterly appearance. As people are apt to pluck twigs as they walk along, I perhaps might do the ſame, and by chance might obſerve, that a *ſingle bud* on that twig had begun to ſwell. I ſhould reaſon very unnaturally, or rather not reaſon at all, to ſuppoſe *this* was the *only* bud in England which had this appearance. Inſtead of deciding thus, I ſhould inſtantly conclude, that the ſame appearance was beginning, or about to begin, every where ; and though the vegetable ſleep will continue longer on ſome trees and plants than on others, and though ſome of them may not *bloſſom* for two or three years, all will be in leaf in the ſummer, except thoſe which are *rotten*. What pace the political ſummer may keep with the natural, no human foreſight can determine. It is, however, not difficult to perceive that the ſpring is begun.—Thus wiſhing, as I ſincerely do, freedom and happineſs to all nations, I cloſe the

SECOND PART.

APPENDIX.

AS the publication of this work has been delayed beyond the time intended, I think it not improper, all circumftances confidered, to ftate the caufes that have occafioned the delay.

The reader will probably obferve, that fome parts in the plan contained in this work for reducing the taxes, and certain parts in Mr. Pitt's fpeech at the opening of the prefent feffion, Tuefday, January 31, are fo much alike, as to induce a belief, that either the Author had taken the hint from Mr. Pitt, or Mr. Pitt from the Author.—I will firft point out the parts that are fimilar, and then ftate fuch circumftances as I am acquainted with, leaving the reader to make his own conclufion.

Confidering it almoft an unprecedented cafe, that taxes fhould be propofed to be taken off, it is equally as extraordinary that fuch a meafure fhould occur to two perfons at the fame time; and ftill more fo, (confidering the vaft variety and multiplicity of taxes) that they fhould hit on the fame fpecific taxes. Mr. Pitt has mentioned, in his fpeech, the tax on *Carts* and *Waggons*—that on *Female Servants*—the lowering the tax on *Candles*, and the taking off the tax of three fhillings on *Houfes* having under feven windows.

Every one of thofe fpecific taxes are a part of the plan contained in this work, and propofed alfo to be taken off. Mr. Pitt's plan, it is true, goes no farther than to a reduction of three hundred and twenty thoufand pounds; and the reduction propofed in this work to nearly fix millions. I have made my calculations on only fixteen millions and a half of revenue, ftill afferting that it was " very " nearly, if not quite, feventeen millions." Mr. Pitt ftates it at 16,690,000. I know enough of the matter to fay, that he has not *overftated* it. Having thus given the particulars, which correfpond in this work and his fpeech, I will ftate a chain of circumftances that may lead to fome explanation.

The firft hint for leffening the taxes, and that as a confequence flowing from the French revolution, is to be found in the ADDRESS and DECLARATION of the Gentlemen who met at the Thatched-Houfe Tavern, Auguft 20, 1791. Among many other particulars ftated in that Addrefs, is the following, put as an interrogation to the govern-

government oppofers of the French Revolution. " *Are* " *they forry that the pretence for new oppreffive taxes, and the* " *occafion for continuing many old taxes will be at an end?*

It is well known, that the perfons who chiefly frequent the Thatched Houfe Tavern, are men of court connections, and fo much did they take this Addrefs and Declaration refpecting the French revolution and the reduction of taxes in difguft, that the Landlord was under the neceffity of informing the Gentlemen, who compofed the meeting of the twentieth of Auguft, and who propofed holding another meeting, that he could not receive them *.

What was only hinted at in the Addrefs and Declaration, refpecting taxes and principles of government, will be found reduced to a regular fyftem in this work. But as Mr. Pitt's fpeech contains fome of the fame things refpecting taxes, I now come to give the circumftances before alluded to.

The cafe is: This work was intended to be publifhed juft before the meeting of Parliament, and for that purpofe a confiderable part of the copy was put into the printer's hands in September, and all the remaining copy, as far as page 160, which contains the parts to which Mr. Pitt's fpeech is fimilar, was given to him full fix weeks before the meeting of parliament, and he was informed of the time at which it was to appear. He had compofed nearly the

whole

---

* The gentleman who figned the addrefs and declaration as chairman of the meeting, M. Horne Tooke, being generally fuppofed to be the perfon who drew it up, and having fpoken much in commendation of it, has been jocularly accufed of praifing his own work. To free him from this embaraffment, and to fave him the repeated trouble of mentioning the author, as he has not failed to do, I make no hefitation in faying, that as the opportunity of benefiting by the French Revolution eafily occurred to me, I drew up the publication in queftion, and fhewed it to him and fome other gentlemen: who, fully approving it, held a meeting for the purpofe of making it public, and fubfcribed to the amount of fifty guineas to defray the expence of advertifing. I believe there are at this time, in England, a greater number of men acting on difinterefted principles, and determined to look into the nature and practices of government themfelves, and not blindly truft, as has hitherto been the cafe, either to government generally, or to parliaments, or to parliamentary oppofition, than at any former period. Had this been done a century ago, corruption and taxation had not arrived to the height they are now at.

Whole about a fortnight before the time of Parliament
meeting, and had printed as far as page 112, and had given
me a proof of the next sheet, up to page 128. It was then
in sufficient forwardness to be out at the time proposed, as
two other sheets were ready for striking off. I had before
told him, that if he thought he should be straightened
for time, I would get part of the work done at another
press, which he desired me not to do. In this manner the
work stood on the Tuesday fortnight preceding the meeting of Parliament, when all at once, without any previous
intimation, though I had been with him the evening before,
he sent me, by one of his workmen, all the remaining
copy, from page 112, declining to go on with the work *on
any consideration.*

To account for this extraordinary conduct I was totally
at a loss, as he stopped at the part where the arguments on
systems and principles of government closed, and where the
plan for the reduction of taxes, the education of children,
and the support of the poor and the aged begins; and still
more especially, as he had, at the time of his beginning to
print, and before he had seen the whole copy, offered a thousand pounds for the copy-right, together with the future
copy-right of the former part of the Rights of Man. I
told the person who brought me this offer that I should not
accept it, and wished it not to be renewed, giving him as
my reason, that though I believed the printer to be an
honest man, I would never put it in the power of any printer
or publisher to suppress or alter a work of mine, by making
him master of the copy, or give to him the right of selling it to
any minister, or to any other person, or to treat as a mere
matter of traffic, that which I intended should operate as a
principle.

His refusal to complete the work (which he could not
purchase) obliged me to seek for another printer, and this
of consequence would throw the publication back till after
the meeting of Parliament, otherways it would have appeared that Mr. Pitt had only taken up a part of the plan
which I had more fully stated.

Whether that gentleman, or any other, had seen the
work, or any part of it, is more than I have authority to
say. But the manner in which the work was returned,
and the particular time at which this was done, and that after
the offers he had made, are suspicious circumstances. I know
what the opinion of booksellers and publishers is upon such
a case, but as to my own opinion, I chuse to make no declaration

N

tion. There are many ways by which proof sheets may be procured by other persons before a work publicly appear, to which I shall add a certain circumstance, which is,

A ministerial bookseller in Piccadilly who has been employed, as common report says, by a clerk of one of the boards closely connected with the ministry (the board of trade and plantation of which Hawksbury is president) to publish what he calls my Life (I wish his own life and that thsoe of the cabinet were as good) used to have his books printed at the same printing-office that I employed; but when the former part of *Rights of Man* came out, he took his work away in dudgeon; and about a week or ten days before the printer returned my copy, he came to make him an offer of his work again, which was accepted. This would consequently give him admission into the printing-office where the sheets of this work were then lying; and as booksellers and printers are free with each other, he would have the opportunity of seeing what was going on. —Be the case however as it may, Mr. Pitt's plan, little and diminutive as it is, would have had a very awkward appearance, had this work appeared at the time the printer had engaged to finish it.

I have now stated the particulars which occasioned the delay, from the proposal to purchase, to the refusal to print. If all the Gentlemen are innocent, it is very unfortunate for them that such a variety of suspicious circumstances should, without any design, arrange themselves together.

Having now finished this part, I will conclude with stating another circumstance.

About a fortnight or three weeks before the meeting of Parliament, a small addition, amounting to about twelve shillings and six pence a year, was made to the pay of the soldiers, or rather, their pay was docked so much less. Some Gentlemen who knew, in part, that this work would contain a plan of reforms respecting the oppressed condition of soldiers, wished me to add a note to the work, signifying, that the part upon that subject had been in the printer's hands some weeks before that addition of pay was proposed. I declined doing this, lest it should be interpreted into an air of vanity, or an endeavour to excite susoicion (for which, perhaps, there might be no grounds) that some of the government gentlemen, had, by some means or other, made out what this work would contain: and had not the printing been interrupted so as to occasion a delay beyond the time fixed for publication, nothing contained in this appendix would have appeared.

THOMAS PAINE.

www.ingramcontent.com/pod-product-compliance
Ingram Content Group UK Ltd.
Pitfield, Milton Keynes, MK11 3LW, UK
UKHW042153280225
455719UK00001B/314